BLACK & BLUE

A journey through the lens of an unapologetic, black female officer

LANAH WRIGHT

ILLUSTRATION BY LANAH WRIGHT

PRINTED IN THE UNITED STATES OF AMERICA

ISBN #

For my daddy, who not only supported me but made me feel like I could accomplish anything. For pushing me to write this book and keeping me motivated. I miss you!

For my mom, sisters, and brother;

For all women in law enforcement, especially black women;

For all fallen officers killed in the line of duty;

For the black and brown lives taken by police brutality; and

For my fellow officers and my former co-workers who encouraged me to write my book.

table of contents

"Don't let other people's opinions distort your reality. Be true to yourself. Be bold in pursuing your dreams.

Be unapologetically you!" –Steve Maraboli

preface

As I sit down to write the beginning of my story, I find myself reflecting on the journey that has brought me here. A journey full of challenges and triumphs, with moments of despair, accompanied by countless experiences that have shaped me into the woman I am today – **an unapologetic, black female police officer.**

To be clear, this is not a story of a victim, nor is it a story of defeat. While there have been some unfavorable experiences that I have dealt with as a **black female police officer**, I have also had some noteworthy ones. This is simply my story: the good, the bad, and the ugly.

This book is a candid collection of experiences shared through mini-stories. In a profession often misunderstood and misrepresented, especially when it comes to people of color and, more specifically, black women, I have strived to be truthful and accurate in representing all the facts as they occurred. I have not changed beginnings or endings to make myself look good or to protect my former department.

Conversely, the location and the names of all individuals included in this book, **from this point on**, are fictional and/or omitted for confidentiality and safety reasons.

In sharing my story, I hope to inspire, to educate, and to challenge perspectives. Most importantly, I hope to give a voice to many unspoken experiences of not only black female officers, but officers of color and female officers everywhere.

introduction

I would've liked to start this book off by saying writing this book was ALL my idea. I found this quote somewhere, probably on Instagram, which read, *"Every word has consequences, Every silence, too."* Powerful right? After reading that quote, I decided it was time for me to share my story.

To say I came up with this brilliant idea to write this book would be a lie. You know what they say, "Never start a relationship on a lie, it always seems to end terribly." I mean, the fact that you purchased this book and have decided to read it makes me feel like this is the beginning of a virtual friendship, and I promise I will be completely honest throughout the book.

Okay, so before you start making speculations about my character and questioning the truth of the stories highlighted below, hear me out.

This is what really happened…

Somewhere in between 2018 - 2019, I was encouraged to write this book. My sergeant tasked my partner and me with working the grand opening event for one of Nick Cannon's rooftop bars. My job was simple: **do not let anyone pass the steel metal barricades unless they have a VIP pass**. I thought, *oooh easy-peasy*!

Since I was tasked with this job by my sergeant, I took it seriously… not in a weird, megalomaniac way. I just didn't want to disappoint him. He is a good guy and a remarkable leader.

Anyhow, for two straight hours, I stood by the steel metal barricades and *policed* who entered the venue. My partner on one end and me on the other. It was actually incredibly boring, and I was beginning to feel this was some sort of punishment.

My back was hurting from standing, and at that very moment, I was instantaneously reminded of a previous job I had in college that required me to stand the entire shift. Just stand, greet people, and open the door for guests when they entered or exited the venue. Incredibly boring! Needless to say, I quit after the first month. I hated it! I would sneak into the dressing rooms just to take a "seated" break. Having to soak my entire body after every shift wasn't cutting it for me.

Okay, I digress. After denying entry to several people who did not have a VIP pass, I started to look like a real, miserable person. People, mostly women, were staring at and mean-mugging me, making comments under their breath like, *"It's not that serious,"* or *"Whoa, you take your job way too seriously,"* all because they weren't able to see Nick Cannon and his "Wild N' Out" crew.

Not gon' lie; if the roles were reversed and I was in the line, dealing with **me**, I too would say something along the lines of, *"Dang, this girl really loves her job. It ain't that serious,"* but I was not, and I like to believe dealing with me is **<u>ALWAYS</u>** a pleasant experience.

After hearing the comments, I smiled and said, "Yup." It wasn't the show-your-teeth smile but more like the closed-lips, gentle smirk. I mean, what can I say? I was given very strict instructions.

So, back to the story…

While I was standing at the steel metal barricades, I saw an older black guy, not extremely old, but older than the rest of the crowd. He looked like he was maybe 45 years old, but you know black don't crack, so he could've been older. This man walked up to the line without a visible security pass, no VIP pass, nothing. He proceeded to cut the line and began to move the barricade… I mean, PHYSICALLY move the barricade in attempts to gain entry.

Every other person who attempted to do that same thing was immediately stopped by myself or my partner. As you can imagine, the same thing was going to happen to this guy.

Right as I was about to tell this guy he needed to stay on the other side of the barricade and wait like everyone else, something prevented me from saying anything. With my eyebrows raised, I stared at him with squinted eyes. My body language, accompanied by my partner's look of disapproval, did not phase him.

"Who is this guy?" I thought.

He smiled and essentially said, "In all my years, I have never seen a young, black female cop, and you're very pretty. I am sure you have seen and experienced a lot." Although I was still stuck on the fact that he disregarded the steel barricade used to deter people from entering, I politely replied, "Thank you."

We talked for about 10 minutes, and during this time, he encouraged me to do a podcast. I laughed as I explained to him how I disliked hearing my voice and wouldn't want to do a solo podcast, I'd need a partner. Those of you who don't like to listen to voice messages and voicemails left by you understand my pain.

Thinking about it now, I haven't had an actual voice message set up for my voicemail since my freshman year of high school when my sister sang on my voicemail. Haha! I know some of y'all remember when that was cool. Shout out to my sister for coming through with the vocals.

This guy was persistent. He reminded me of how important my story was, even though he knew nothing about me. After a brief pause, he asked, "What about a book?"

"A book? Definitely doable," I replied. He explained to me people need to hear my story, *the good, the bad, and the ugly.*

So here I am. Here we are!

Oh, and the guy I met, the one without a security pass or VIP pass visible as instructed, the one that planted that seed to write my book, was Mr. James Cannon, Nick Cannon's father. Mr. Cannon has responded to my yearly text messages about my book and has continued to encourage me.

So, thank you for believing in me, Mr. Cannon.

<u>PART I:</u>

unapologetically **BLACK**

"I am the dream and the hope of the slave."
Maya Angelou

Lanah Wright

unapologetically **BLACK**

"how it all started…"

You're probably wondering how I ended up ~~in this situation~~ … **well no, with this job**… yes, that's more like it. Well, there were two significant incidents in my life that prompted me to change my major from sociology to international crime and justice.

the traffic stop

It was a gloomy, rainy day *(All good stories start like this, but it really was a gloomy, rainy day)*. We were driving southbound on Ninth Street; well, actually, I wasn't driving. I was sitting in the rear passenger seat of my friend's vehicle. It was pouring rain, might I add, and we were headed to grab food for the evening. I was in college at the time. My friend, a black male, was driving, and our friend, a black female, was seated in the front passenger seat.

Like I was saying, it was pouring rain. The sky was a tar-black color with large dark gray clouds. The clouds looked like they were coming at me. Loud-sounding pitter-patter was hitting the windows. The streets were becoming flooded with water, and loose gravel began to fill the potholes.

While sitting in the back, I noticed a flash of red and blue lights illuminating from behind me. I looked through the rearview mirror and saw a marked patrol vehicle positioned behind us. After a few deep breaths, I nervously said, "Great, we are being pulled over." In a deep, demanding male voice, I heard, "Relax!" *Umm okay?* I thought.

There was a moment of silence as we began to pull the car to the right. So much tension you would think we had something illegal inside of the vehicle. We were good college students. I had just started college. A freshman. They were both juniors in their third year of school.

My heart began to pound as I watched two white male officers exit their marked patrol vehicle and begin to approach our car. The officer on the left side of the vehicle began tapping the driver-side window while simultaneously instructing us to exit the vehicle.

Huh? Okay, I know this was not normal protocol, but I was also outnumbered. From the backseat, I politely asked the white male officer, "Why do we have to get out of the vehicle?" "Be quiet, Lanah," my female friend stuttered while demanding my silence. *Wow. I was outnumbered.*

He yelled, "Get out of the car!!!" Well, it was either a yell or just a raising of his voice. I've been told I often get those two confused. Either way, his tone was not pleasant. My friends and I exited the vehicle.

At this point, we were standing in the rain. Each raindrop that hit my face trickled down to my clothing and began to soak through my shirt. Shivering, I watched as vehicles sped by, loose gravel being kicked up by the tires of those vehicles. I began memorizing the officers' last names while attempting to embrace the cold and discomfort. "I'm going to complain about this," I whispered to my friend. She ignored me. *Why isn't anyone upset about this?*

I realized these officers didn't care much about protecting and serving the community they policed. Instead, they thrived on control.

The same white male officer who was tapping on the driver's side window quickly walked back toward us and yelled, "Are you throwing rocks at us?" Now this… this was, in fact, a yell. "MEEEEE?" I asked. "Yeah, you," he quickly replied. Confused, I responded, "Um, no." I wanted to ask,

"Are you dumb? You don't see the cars speeding by you, kicking up the loose gravel. Idiot!" I didn't. I just miserably stood there in silence. Soaked.

They completed the search of my friend's vehicle and sent him off with a ticket. The reason for searching the vehicle was unknown. I thought. No, no, no, this can't be within their policies and procedures. We need to complain.

Sadly, I didn't have enough knowledge of search and seizures, laws of arrests, or vehicle traffic stops and detentions, so I could not complain. I didn't feel properly armed and equipped to complain about the violation of our Fourth Amendment rights, so I let it go. We drove home in silence. We didn't even pick up food.

the assault

I was assaulted. I don't want to go into the details because I have worked through this, and it's just too heavy for this book. However, what I can say is I know how it feels to call the police for what was an emergency and receive an incurious response from responding officers. This was it.

I had two unpleasant experiences, both during my undergraduate career. So, I switched my major from sociology to criminal justice in my second year of college. As you will later read in upcoming chapters, there was a lot of thought put into my switch, but I did it.

Here is the "cliff notes[1]" version.

I chose to become a police officer to be a positive role model for women, especially black women. I wanted to be the officer I never saw when I was younger to inspire others. I know how it feels to be treated disrespectfully by law

---

[1] Quick summary and/or short basic analysis of something.

enforcement officers. I understand how easy it is to become complacent, but I chose to become a police officer to disrupt that cycle.

I chose to take an oath to protect and serve my community while I am in a position of authority. I made a vow to myself that I would use my voice, my knowledge, and my experiences to help bridge the gap between the community and law enforcement.

I realize that whatever happens to ANY OF US, affects ALL OF US, which is why I have chosen to break my silence. I have worked hard to get to where I am today, competing with classmates - *mostly white*, in a school specialized in criminal justice. I have competed with police recruits - *mostly white males*, have been challenged by co-workers - *mostly white males*, and have been doubted in my capabilities when applying for positions within the police department – *by mostly men.* Although I will continue to be conscious of these issues, I refuse to remain silent because my silence has not benefited me.

So, who am I, you ask? I am not a well-known, best-selling author *(...yet).* I am simply an individual who has decided to share her journey as a **black female police officer** because I have learned throughout the years all it takes is the voice of **_one_** to disrupt a group of silent people.

"sticks and stones"

My first thought was, I definitely don't look like a rat. He yelled this after I attempted to put him in a taxi cab INSTEAD of taking him to a sobering center for being drunk in public. This guy was asleep, passed out in a pedicab[2]. The pedicab operator flagged me down, requesting my assistance. His exact words were, "There is a male passed out in the back of my pedicab." My partner and I walked over, and sure enough, the male was passed out in the back of his pedicab.

I am way too familiar with how abruptly waking someone up could end up being an extremely unpleasant experience for both parties, so instead, I attempted to gently wake the male up by softly tapping his shoulder and announcing, "Police, wake up."

After a few soft shakes, I watched as he opened his eyes; confused, of course, I immediately said, "I can see you've had a little too much to drink; it's time to go home. Let's order you an Uber." When he responded, I noticed his speech was slurred. I could smell the odor of an alcoholic beverage emanating from his breath.

He kept repeating, "Okay, I'll just drive home. I just need my dog." The pedicab operator quickly interjected by yelling, "What dog? You didn't have a dog! You got in a fistfight with some guy and tried to get in your car and drive away, that's why I have your keys. No dog! No dog!"

---

[2] A small pedal-operated vehicle, serving as a taxi in some countries

Although you may not see it now, I made a huge effort to avoid taking this guy to jail. I instructed the male a second time to order an Uber. He showed me a wad of cash and told me he could take a taxi.

I believe in chances. He had one chance to prove he was able to care for himself. Technically, it is not a crime to be drunk, but when you are unable to care for yourself and you're drunk in a public place it becomes a safety issue, and you are now a liability.

I flagged down a taxi and stayed until the taxi drove off to ensure the intoxicated male remained inside the taxi.

Perfect, he remained inside of the taxi. I watched as the taxi driver proceeded to head northbound on Eighth Avenue.

As soon as I turned my back and began walking in the opposite direction, the sound of loud honking and horns blaring began to fill the air.

"BEEEEEEEPPP BEEEEEEEEEEEP." I looked toward where the loud, incessant honking noise was coming from and saw the **same** intoxicated Middle Eastern male I **just** assisted into the taxi. He was standing in the middle of the street, causing a hazard. A calm evening now turned into a chaotic, overwhelming atmosphere. A loud high pitched *"BEEEEPPP"* came from behind me. Drivers loudly honking their horns while trying to avoid hitting this intoxicated male. Welp, now we have an issue.

At this point, I realized he needed to go to our sobering center because he was clearly unable to care for himself. My partner and I walked toward him. While he was still of calm demeanor, I instructed him to place his hands behind his back and advised him he was under arrest for being drunk in public.

He complied by slowly placing his hands behind his back. As soon, and I mean as soon as those handcuffs went on both wrists, he turned to look toward me and said, "Ma'am, please…please, I helped your people."

My people? I laughed. "What does that have to do with you being drunk in public? I gave you multiple opportunities to go home." He responded, "I work at the gas station. I always help your people." Already knowing the answer, I questioned, "Who are my people?" He quietly mumbled, "You know, the black people." I laughed and simply responded, "Okay," as I escorted him into the back of my patrol vehicle.

From the back seat of the patrol vehicle, he began using both feet to kick the rear windows of the patrol vehicle while yelling, ***"You rat b*tch, I helped your people!"***

This was pretty creative, you know, adding **rat** in front of an already extremely derogatory, offensive name to call someone.

After all this, I was glad I took this intoxicated male to jail. There you have it; he spent the night in jail. I call that a win! Wouldn't you? I mean, by the end of the night he was clearly unable to care for himself.

No, STOP! I know what you're thinking, and you think I arrested him because he called me a *"rat b*tch"* or suggested he helped *"my people."*

You see, if you go back to the start of this interaction I tried to reason with this guy. I tried to send this guy home in a taxi but he just wouldn't leave. As you read, he was clearly unable to care for himself.

Keep it 100 though…I definitely don't think I look like a rat. How rude!

Tip: *No matter how triggered you may feel, you will never be able to reason with someone who is intoxicated.*
Don't waste your time!

CUTEST
RAT
B*TCH
EVER!

Ta-Da! Now, that was a small glimpse of how this book will be. Throughout my book, I promise to be completely honest and candid. I refuse to hold anything back. I recognize there will be portions of this book that may be heavy. Given the topics discussed, it is possible the certain readers, such as white readers, officers who choose to remain silent, individuals who lack respect for law enforcement, especially women in law enforcement, may have moments of discomfort.

Don't stop reading when it gets uncomfortable. Keep an open mind and challenge yourself to truly see things from a different perspective, my perspective. Again, this is my reality. Keep in mind that I am not a professor, poet, or educator. I am a police officer with a voice.

All **TIPS*** included after each highlighted situation were formed from my experiences, strictly my modest opinion or, shall I say, my "two cents."

The illustrations included in this book, well, those are for you, by me. Illustrating pieces of this book was a healing activity. For the sections I felt led to draw, I did just that. I drew whatever came to mind. Pretty cathartic and therapeutic, if you ask me.

"sticks and stones"

> *"You're just a house nigger…you Uncle Tom nigger." –*
> *Biracial, 35-year-old light-skinned male*

Says the light-skinned, biracial, intoxicated male, who was the subject of multiple noise complaints that evening. I laughed because this was honestly the first time I have been called a "house nigger." I mean, I've been called a nigger, a nigga, a nigger cunt, but not a house nigger. To be called this by a light-skinned male, who could be perceived as white, which in itself carries way more status, was new to me.

I remember reading about *"House Negros and Field Negros"* in an article highlighting a speech delivered by *Malcolm X,* or maybe it was from one of his speeches I watched, I can't recall. I do however believe, the historical term for a "house negro" is one who is of higher status than a "field negro." I guess because I am a black officer, I should view myself as someone of higher status because I have submerged myself in a profession that employs predominately white males. Not true, but I guess I can understand his thought process.

After he called me a ***"house nigger"*** I politely said, I think you got it wrong. I would technically be a "field negro" You are a lighter complexion than me; you'd probably be in the house.

You are probably asking yourself, *"Can she say that?"* Why yes…yes, I can. I truly don't see anything wrong with that. I was just educating this guy so he didn't make a fool of himself a second time.

He requested to speak to my sergeant to file a complaint because he didn't like my response. While waiting for my sergeant to arrive, he began yelling extremely sexual and derogatory comments toward me. Comments suggesting that I get on my knees for all my white male co-workers, who were standing next to me. He pretty much said every colorful derogatory term around the sun. Just imagine it. I don't think it needs to be repeated. Some things are just better left unsaid. As my grandma used to say, "Leave something for the imagination," so I will do just that.

I stood there, waiting for my sergeant to arrive. Luckily, my body-worn camera was activated during the entire contact. I had nothing to hide.

Once my sergeant arrived, the light-skinned biracial male requested to speak to a black sergeant so that he could file the complaint. That is not how it works, buddy.

Needless to say, he continued yelling very sexual, derogatory comments toward me. Just me. He ignored my white male coworkers, who were, of course, silent.

After standing there for what felt like an eternity, I said, "Either you file the complaint with this sergeant, or you can leave and keep the noise down. You can't pick and choose who you want to speak with because of their race."

The light-skinned biracial male yelled, "Stupid b*tch," as he picked up his belongings and began walking away.

Lucky for me, all the verbal abuse was witnessed by my sergeant and co-workers. No complaints were sustained, and the **House vs. Field negro** comment was never brought up again. Not even by my white co-workers, the ones who chose to remain silent.

> *Tip: Sometimes self-care looks like politely telling them off and adding a lil' bit of education. Don't give their verbal attacks and insults power.*

"sticks and stones"

"Stupid Nigger, why don't you go back to Africa" –
Transient 40–45-year-old white male

This was actually one of the first times a white male was bold enough to call me a **Nigger** while I was on duty. Unbeknownst to me, this would be far from the last.

He yelled that while being handcuffed, sitting in the back of my patrol vehicle. I had just completed the field evaluation and we were headed to jail. He was placed under arrest for being under the influence of a controlled substance; I'm pretty sure it was methamphetamine or "meth." This dude was tripping.

Prior to my contact with him, he was caught stealing items from a local convenience store. Loss prevention officers detained him before my arrival, and of course, they wanted to press charges for the recovered items that totaled around **$5.00** *Rolling my eyes* I mean $5.00? Let it go! Okay, that's not right, stealing is stealing, but I mean, I am not putting my life at risk over **$5.00** of junk food. C'mon!

When I arrived to the scene at the convenience store, the male had clearly just smoked some meth. He was rapidly rambling, his lips were chapped, visibly painfully chapped, his eyes were bloodshot red, and he was sweating profusely. I performed a field evaluation to determine whether or not my assumptions were correct. The evaluation confirmed my assumptions.

Let's fast forward through to the part where he told me to go back to Africa. I think he was hit with the realization that he was actually going to jail while he was handcuffed, and two officers in uniform were driving him. Or maybe it could've been because he was coming down from his high…who knows? Anyways, he started by calling me a monkey and continued his show by adding that I had ugly, big lips.

I actually love my lips, so commenting about my lips was not going to phase me. *A monkey?* You have to come harder than that. I laughed and continued driving. I could see he was getting a bit frustrated that his comments weren't bothering me. During the series of these events, my field training officer[3] sat in the passenger seat of the vehicle, quiet. Not a word was said…**nothing.**

A few seconds later, the white male yelled, ***"Stupid Nigger, why don't you go back to Africa."***

The car enveloped displeasing quietness. That awkward silence created in itself an intense feeling of inescapable tension. My field training officer's body language displayed his discomfort. I watched him through my peripheral vision as he extended his left arm, reached for the dial on the radio, and turned up the volume. Still, not one word was said. Nope… no *"That's enough,"* or *"Knock it off,"* or even, *"Okay bro, chill,"* and it was at that very moment I realized I was on my own.

Nonetheless, I thought about ignoring his comment, but I just could not resist. I replied, "Wow, I've never been to Africa, but I would love to go someday." I don't think he expected a response. He immediately said, "Yeah, you should go so you can work the plantations." I smiled and said, "Okay, sir." At this point, I believe he ran out of fuel. He was subsequently booked into jail without any issues.

---

[3] An experienced senior police officer who is responsible for training and evaluating new officers while they are in their probationary period.

He didn't say anything else until we got to jail. I'm not sure if he ran out of racist comments or insulting me no longer amused him. Either way it goes, I want to say I won…but that would be biased, huh?

*Tip: Like my dad used to say, "In this life, we or <u>YOU</u> will have two thoughts. One negative to yourself and others; the other positive. YOU have the power, through Christ, to accept one and throw out the other, JUST LIKE THE UNWANTED MAIL YOU GET EVERY DAY." This also applies to comments made by others. **Throw it out.***

Blah, blah, blah...

"patrolling: it's not just BLACK & white"

"C'mon, sis, why are you doing this to us? You can let me go"- 25–30-year-old black male.

Are you kidding me? I think this is one of the things that tends to bother me the most. You're probably wondering why… hopefully not, but if you are, I'll give you my opinion on it.

What I dislike the most are the individuals who expect a pass. What would you like a pass from? A pass from committing a crime, breaking the law, or being dumb? No! You don't get a pass.

This 25-30-year-old black male was fighting in public and expected a pass because he saw a black officer respond to the scene. Instead of owning up to his actions, he was hoping he was not going to be held responsible and felt a black officer was going to be his saving grace. *This was my assumption* Either way, it does not work like that.

While I do believe everyone makes mistakes, there comes a time when you really need to take some responsibility; it's part of the process of growing up. I'm sure we have all heard that as a child, and if not, I am telling you now…

TAKE RESPONSIBILITY FOR YOUR ACTIONS!

To be honest he should respect that I am holding him accountable for his actions. Maybe he'll learn…hopefully, it'll help change his mindset.

While passively resisting when my partner and I were placing him in handcuffs he looked at me and said, ***"C'mon, sis, why are you doing this to us? You can let me go."*** I respectfully asked, "You want me to let you go?" He smiled and replied, "Yeah." I smiled and asked, "Would you be okay if I let someone go after they repeatedly punched and kicked you in the head? I didn't receive a response. Just dead silence.

As you may have expected, he went to jail that night. After punching the guy in the face, causing him to fall to the ground, this 25–30-year-old black male proceeded to kick the guy in the head. You may have guessed all this was likely to cause great bodily injury to the individual who was assaulted.

Right is right and wrong is wrong. I can't do work from the inside if I am not holding everyone to the same standard.

I know there are times when I tend to apply the "spirit of the law[4]" rather than the "letter of the law[5]," but it is for minor violations, like rolling through a stop sign, speeding on a freeway, or texting while driving.

These are situations where you can be educated and let off with a warning. These situations are completely different than the incident I highlighted above, which is why I could not just let him off with a warning.

---

[4] To follow the intention of why the law was enforced. Leaves room for officer discretion.

[5] To follow the literal meaning of the law and punishment that follows. No room for exceptions or interpretation.

33

> **Tip:** *If you are ever in a position like this, take moments like these to educate. Let them know we are not the enemy. A crime is a crime. Education is key.*

"patrolling: it's not just BLACK & white"

*"**Don't arrest me, I like black people**" –30- year-old white male.*

Taken aback, I softly giggled when I heard this. To prevent myself from allowing my giggle to turn into a full-blown laugh, I quickly composed myself. We were dealing with a serious matter and it was not the time, nor the place for laughter.

Let me guess…*you've dated a black girl before…*or wait, no, *you have a black best friend*? I really wanted to ask him. I mean, I was curious. Instead, with my practiced poker face, I replied, "Sir, in this state, domestic violence is taken very seriously. Throughout my preliminary investigation, I believe you were the main aggressor in this incident."

After a slight pause, he replied, "I didn't do anything. I didn't hurt her. ***Please don't arrest me, I like black people.***" My partner and I placed him in handcuffs. He didn't say he liked white people, just black people. Why?

I'm sure you're reading this and thinking to yourself, *"Girl this did not happen, there is no way it happened.* Ha! It did, which motivated me to write this book. So, shoutout to all of you for providing me with such great material for this book; you are making it way too easy.

Nonetheless, the white male who choked and hit his girlfriend after a heated argument went to jail for domestic violence.

Sadly, one thing I have noticed working in this field is how often we respond to domestic violence incidents. Each incident is different, but I found that thousands of men and women have been abused by their partners or significant others.

Whether it's emotional, verbal, or physical, if you're reading this and feel you're stuck in an abusive domestic violence cycle, the best thing you can do is seek help.

YOU ARE NOT ALONE!

Tip: Domestic Violence Hotline
1 (800) 799.SAFE (7233) | TTY
1.800.787.3224

"the token"

*"**Did you go to the Ice Cube concert this weekend?**" a 45-year-old white sergeant*

I want to start by saying I love the department I work for; I truly do. The following situation does not represent every officer or sergeant I work with, which is why it is important to note that my sergeant's actions do not represent the actions of all officers. However, as promised, I am going to keep it real with you all; I do believe there are some racist, ignorant officers, but I do not believe all officers are racist. I mean, that would be a bit anecdotal.

Anyhow, you better watch out; they could be your supervisors one day.

Dun Dun Dun...

On most days, after line-up, I would make my way to the evidence room to stock up on gloves and any equipment needed in preparation for my shift. While a few of my co-workers were engaged in idle chatter, I went to the computer to submit my timecard and respond to any emails that I missed during my off days.

Despite the clacking of the keyboard and my undivided attention to the task at hand, which was my emails, I saw my sergeant enter the evidence room. I continued to focus on my emails until I felt this weird sensation as if I was being watched. When I lifted my head and allowed my eyes to leave the computer screen, there was this momentary freeze on my behalf. He was staring at me.

Weirdo! We locked eyes. Of course, it was the uncomfortable locking of eyes. It kind of felt like somewhat of an intrusion into my personal space.

While looking at my sergeant, I noticed his mouth begin to slightly open, as if he was getting ready to speak. He had this strange look on his face. It was a look someone makes when they're getting ready to comment on something you said earlier, believing that their comment would be really good, like something clever or funny. If you were able to visualize that face I just described, that's the one.

At this point, it was still quiet. I didn't say anything and he did not make any comments…yet. I immediately started asking myself, *"Did you categorize all of your body-worn camera videos? Did you complete your report from last night? Did you miss court?"* All these questions were thoughts going through my head.

After what felt like five minutes of awkward silence, my sergeant looked at me and asked, "Hey, how was your weekend?" I quickly replied, "It was good. I didn't do anything, just relaxed."

After I JUST told my sergeant I didn't do ANYTHING, he smiled and asked, ***"Did you go to the Ice Cube concert?"***

HOLD UP! WAIT A MINUTE! DID I WHAT?

Puzzled. Confused. Confounded. I thought to myself, *Nah, I didn't go to the damn Ice Cube concert!* Now, this is how I wanted to respond, but I bit my tongue, as I normally tend to do.

I continued this dialogue in my head before even responding. *You think just because I am black I went to the Ice Cube concert to support a black artist or I must strike you as someone who listens to rap because I am black.* No offense to Ice Cube. I do like his music, but that's not the point. The ignorance of this man and I say ignorance because I don't think he's a bad person; I don't necessarily hate the guy. The issue is his lack of knowledge, cultural awareness, and understanding…or maybe he is racist. It was too soon to tell.

I'm sure you're wondering what happened next after the unpleasant silence. Well, nothing really. Such an anticlimactic ending, huh?

I mean I did respond after I collected my thoughts and composed myself by replying with a lie, "No. I actually don't like Ice Cube. Why would you think I did?" My white sergeant fretfully replied, "Oh no, I was just wondering."

I know… I know…very passive-aggressive on my end, but I enjoyed making this white sergeant feel uncomfortable. It's annoying, but I chose to pick my battles. I have now spent five years learning how to navigate in a predominantly white male profession. Trust me, it ain't easy.

Oh, and if you're reading this Ice Cube, I do like your music and your work. You're very talented! I lied to prove a point.

---

*Tip: **BREATHE DEEP** & pick your battles.
Passive aggression can be appropriate in certain settings.
Haters will tell you otherwise.*

"the token"

"I've never been attracted to a black woman. You're the first." –28-year-old white male co-worker

Normally, I do not hang out with my co-workers on the weekends. This time is designated for my family and non-law enforcement friends. On this particular day, I decided to meet up with one of my friends, who also happened to be my co-worker.

We were having a nice lunch, off duty. He was one of the few people I considered a friend in the department. Typically when I am off duty, I try and talk about anything, but the job. I mean, who wants to talk about work while being off duty? It's a break from work. Well, actually, you'd be surprised how many officers love talking about work on the weekends. This is either the most exciting thing about their lives or the only thing they have in common with one another. I get it! I have been there. You probably forgot I am a cop, but this isn't my life. This is my profession. There's a difference.

Anyway.

While we were talking about everything but cop stuff, he started telling me he had been attracted to me for a while, then proceeded to say, ***"I've never been attracted to a black woman; you're the first."***

I guess this was meant to be a compliment from his side, and I know a lot of black women have gone through this at least ten times in their lives. I do, kind of believe these racial micro-aggressions are messages usually sent to us by well-intentioned white people.

Maybe? I guess. I don't know. Sometimes sent by well-intentioned white people. Those other times…I guess just by white people.

I do believe most of the time they are not aware of the hidden messages that are being sent verbally, so let's [as in YOU white people] become more aware. At this point, **there are NO excuses. It's dehumanizing and ridiculously ignorant.**

Let's start seeing black female law enforcement officers as equals. Let's, as in **YOU READING THIS BOOK**, start seeing black women as equals. PERIOD! We are human. Just like you! Please confront your unconscious biases.

Oh, and WE, meaning us black women, need to stop brushing comments like these off. I know I am guilty of it. I think there is a human desire to feel included and represented, but acting as if these comments are compliments is only hurting us and leading us to believe it is okay when it is not.

I'm sure he thought he was complimenting me, but I explained to him it was not a compliment but just the opposite. We had a conversation about it. He listened and was receptive. And need I tell you that it was refreshing.

We are still friends today. He checked himself and has since become a great white ally. I have witnessed him unlearn harmful behaviors and his unconscious biases while recognizing his privilege as not only a white man, but a white man who holds power as a police officer.

See! Not all officers are corrupt, and not all white officers are racist. We, as black women and men, need to understand we can't effect any change from the inside on our own. We need our allies. We need real support. This right here is what support looks like to me.

Our relationship remained strictly amicable, and we remained friends.

Tip: *We need to strive to lift one another up, not tear each other down. Let's make every effort to educate not only people in our communities, but also men and women in law enforcement who believe the color of your skin dictates your beauty, intelligence, and importance.*

"the token"

"Can I ask you something, ma'am? Why did you want to be a cop...especially being black?" – 21-year-old black male (Driver of a 2016 Mercedes)

While standing at the intersection of Broadway and A Street, a loud screech of tires alerted everyone on foot, including my partner and me. As I turned my head toward the noise, I saw a black 2016 Mercedes being driven at an accelerated rate of speed toward pedestrians. The driver of the 2016 Mercedes careened through the stop sign, narrowly missing a large group of pedestrians, causing them to jump back onto the curb, a place of safety.

As I loudly gasped, I heard the sound of their gasps as they realized they could have been hit. I had no choice but to conduct a traffic stop of this black 2016 Mercedes. This driver seemed to have no regard for human life.

I normally hate traffic control. I hate enforcing traffic violations, unless the driver is intoxicated or is putting other pedestrians or drivers on the road in danger.

Fun fact: I got my driver's license permit when I turned 16. I remember my dad forcing me to take the test after I took Driver's Ed at 15. In this after-school course, I read an article titled, *"Motor vehicles are the leading cause of death for U.S. teens."*

For that reason, I preferred riding the transit buses with my friends, but at 16, it was my turn. I passed my test. My parents bought me a car for Christmas the following year. I mean, I think my younger sister was more excited than me. The content of that article lived rent-free in my mind. Additionally, my mom always told me, *"You have to remember you are not only driving for yourself, but you now have to drive for others."* I reflected on that statement and often thought to myself, *"Driving is overwhelming. Now, driving for everyone else on the road is crazy."* I now have to avoid getting hit by someone who is not paying attention. I shouldn't have to worry about this. I am only 16.

My teenage fear fueled my traffic stops. Like I said, I conduct traffic stops on drivers who have done something egregious.

I mean, I speed. I am guilty of the notorious rolling stops. It's like if I look left, right, and left again slightly before I get to the stop sign, why must I wait an extra minute? C'mon! I don't always signal when I should. I am not above the law, so I try to be fair.

But this…watching the driver of this 2016 Mercedes almost collide with multiple pedestrians, now that was something concerning. Something that definitely needed my intervention.

As I got inside my patrol vehicle, I was able to catch up to him and safely conduct the traffic stop. The driver of the Mercedes immediately yielded. He wasn't intoxicated. He was just a young black teenager, speeding through a busy intersection downtown, trying to flex[6] in this Mercedes.

---

[6] To show off, to gloat, or to boast.

It must have been his first car, I thought. He had the top down as he was blasting Drake. After pulling him over and talking to him, I issued him a citation. However, I did not cite him for every traffic law he violated; that way, he had the ability to go to traffic school and was able to avoid high fees.

Also, you see, I said I talked to him because that's what I did. I never lecture. Why? I hate being pulled over and being lectured. Give me the ticket, or let me off with a warning. You can't have your cake and eat it too. *Why do people even say that? Wouldn't you want to eat the cake you have?* I never understood the literal meaning of this idiom. Anyway, I try to practice what I preach. For all the traffic officers reading this…we don't need a lecture.

As my partner and I began to walk away, he softly mumbled, ***"Can I ask you something, ma'am? Why did you want to be a cop…especially being black?"***

Ummmmm, *"Ma'am?" How old do I look?* I was only a few years older than him at that time, but you know, it was probably the way I carried myself in uniform. It was definitely giving mature vibes.

After much thought, I confidently answered, "Honestly, I was tired of complaining about local cops and even more tired of not seeing anyone who looked like me on the other side, so I decided to apply. I knew I wanted to make a difference in the world, but I never really had a plan on how. Becoming an officer granted me the opportunity to effect change from the inside."

I watched as he quickly moved his head in an up-and-down motion, nodding in agreement as he smiled and replied, "That's deep."

> ***Tip:*** *We tend to forget an officer is a public servant. We are public servants. Let's use our platform as public servants to make a difference in people's lives.*

"the token"

"This rapper, Tee Grizzley, will be downtown this weekend. He has a bunch of gun charges and stuff. Have you heard of him?" —45-year-old white sergeant

For two years, I worked on a proactive unit that worked primarily downtown in the entertainment district of my city. Downtown was always lit[7]. On Fridays and Saturdays, we could expect different artists headlining clubs.

In addition to policing, I was tasked with keeping track of artists who were coming into town each weekend. To keep track, I would draft a calendar for the upcoming months and send the calendar to my sergeant. I guess it kind of made sense why he would ask me. It was not just the fact that I was the only black officer on the team…right?

For all other talent, like Calvin Harris, Steve Aoki, or any non-black artists or DJs, he would pose the question to the group and look around the table. For questions about any rapper or black artist he would immediately turn to me. You could almost always count on him to mispronounce the artist's name as well. It would take all of me to avoid correcting him. I mean, that would blow my cover, though.

The evening of Tee Grizzley's performance, we were sitting around the line-up table, going over everyone's assignment for the night.

---

[7] According to Merriam-Webster the word lit used in an adjective form was slang meant to describe 1) someone affected by alcohol: Drunk or 2) Excellent or Exciting. Judging by the energy displayed in the party room, it is safe to say the party was *lit.*

He pulled up the event calendar, looked at me, and said, ***"This rapper Tee Grizzley will be downtown this weekend; he has a bunch of gun charges and stuff. Have you heard of him?"***

Mind you, this was the same thing that happened when YG, The Game, and 50 Cent had showings at one of the local clubs downtown.

Instead of growing angry and trying extremely hard to refrain from showing any offense, I responded, "No, not really. Let's play one of his songs to see what he talks about."

This is where the passive aggression came into play. I knew who Tee Grizzley was, and I knew just the right song to scare this middle-aged white sergeant.

I acted as if I was searching for a song, knowing dang well I had already made my decision. I walked toward the computer screen, which projected our call signs and assignments for our shift.

I asked, "Do you mind if we watch a clip of the video, just so we know what we are up against. Just in case we need to patrol that area?" My sergeant cheerfully replied, "Yes, oh absolutely."

Wait, do any of you find it odd when someone replies "Yes" when you ask if they mind? He meant "No" but said yes, which is pretty common.

Within seconds, I pulled up… **"First Day Out"** a classic scare. It was in no way meant to truly scare him, but I guess I secretly wanted to see his reaction. I know we live in a world where people, even law enforcement, have this idea and tend to market black people, especially black men as criminals. Being an insider in the police department, I see it ALL THE TIME. Being a daughter, granddaughter, cousin, niece, and friend to black men, I see it ALL THE TIME.

Wait, have you heard of the myth of the dangerous black man? In a speech or maybe an article by Michelle Alexander, Author of ***"The New Jim Crow: Mass Incarceration in the Age of Colorblindness,"*** she essentially spoke about the cultural production of the ***"dangerous black male"*** and how the myth has been recycled in our culture. Now, don't quote me; I came across this while in graduate school a few years ago. It was something that stuck with me, and I remember Michelle Alexander because I rarely saw black women being highlighted in my courses. See, I was paying attention, Mr. Heffernan.

So, on this day, I saw how terrified my sergeant was of black men. We never spent this much time discussing who the artists were and if they had a criminal background, not since YG came into town.

I showed the video to my sergeant and my squad, which consisted of all white men. For those of you who have never seen this music video, it begins with a cameo of Tee Grizzley wearing an orange suit with "INMATE" inscribed in black across the top left side of the shirt. Behind Tee Grizzley is a bob wire fence and a sign that reads,

"DETROIT REENTRY CENTER MICHIGAN DEPARTMENT OF CORRECTIONS."

The video played, and Tee Grizzley rapped,

*"These n*ggas prayed on my downfall. These n*ggas prayed on my downfall. On all ten, bitch I stood tall. Show these disloyal n*ggas how to ball. Go get a thermometer for the pot, I need this sh*t cooked right. Let's keep this water 400 degrees Fahrenheit. You ever been inside a federal courtroom? N*gga you ever went to trial and fought for your life?"*

Focused and tuned in to my sergeant's reaction, I noticed his mouth was hanging wide open, he appeared to be frozen in time, in a state of surprise or maybe disbelief. I fast-forwarded the video, stopping here…

*"Shoot the smile off your face, I don't joke with n*ggas. Boy I can't trust you with that strap if you don't got no bodies. Boy I can't take you on no lick if you ain't robbed nobody. You ain't no shooter, you can't do that sh*t without no molly."*

That did it. He panicked. I said, "He's a rapper. It's just a song." He apprehensively replied, "No, we are going to need extra patrol at bar break." I don't really know if he was nervous. Although he appeared to be, but never blatantly shared that with me. Why would he?

A few of my fellow white co-workers were in on it. They knew I was going to show this video. They understood the assignment. We parked an empty patrol vehicle at the club where Tee Grizzley was supposed to perform. When the club was closing, he specifically requested that my partner and I respond to that club for more police presence.

We responded. My partner and I stood there and watched as my sergeant attempted to get us to approach every group of black men and women who exited the club and stood on the sidewalk talking. He would say, "They are arguing. That's a good contact." I responded, "They're just talking. Probably waiting for an Uber."

Needless to say, nothing happened. Tee Grizzley showed up at the club and left. No fights. No shootings. Nothing. I love that. I love when we can prove them wrong.

Oh yeah. This was the same sergeant who asked me if I went to the Ice Cube concert.

***Tip:** Pick your battles. You're going to deal with ignorant people wherever you go. Speak up when necessary. Scare them for fun.*
Try it.

"behind the badge"

I began writing this chapter with the idea that I would include a few of the most difficult experiences I've encountered while being an **unapologetic BLACK** police officer.

A few experiences turned to six, six turned to seven, and I found myself deleting some of my experiences because they just came to be too much, too triggering, and too overwhelming. I mean, how can you truly rank difficult racial experiences?

While I don't want to make false promises that this chapter won't be triggering for some, the reality is that if I choose to avoid telling my truth for the comfort of readers, it wouldn't be doing anybody any justice, especially during these difficult, trying times.

The next few experiences I share deserve some type of segue, some nifty transition, or a nice introduction to the new topic. Sadly, I can't think of anything at the moment.

We're about to get into some real stuff, and if the discussions on the topic of racism, race inequality, and social injustices make you feel uncomfortable, and if hearing people say BLACK LIVES MATTER offends you, then you can go ahead and close this book now. ***Ah Ah Ah…actually, don't close the book, I'm joking***.

I spent too much time trying to gather my thoughts and respectfully put them on paper during this civil unrest. I ask that you just read with an open mind. Read with an understanding that while I am a police officer, I am black.

My blackness will always come first.

*"I have a dream that my little children will one day live in a nation where they will not be judged by the color of their skin, but by the content of their character"-****Martin Luther King Jr.***

I used to stand in my parent's living room and would recite this over and over again while staring at the flames inside the fireplace. I listened to the crackling and popping noises coming from the fire. My mom would make sure that I got it right. I was about eight or nine, so I didn't truly know what it meant, but I knew I had to memorize it for my elementary school presentation. I knew I was the only black girl in my class, and besides my siblings and one other girl, we were the only black kids at this private school.

What I didn't know at that age, was we had yet to experience what it felt like to live in a nation where we were not judged by the color of our skin.

Dr. Martin Luther King Jr. delivered his speech on August 28, 1963. Over 30 YEARS before, little ole me began to memorize pieces of his speech.

Fast forward to today, and we still haven't got it right.

Who would've known 2020 would be the most televised year of racial injustice and racial tension? Well, I mean, I think it was the most televised year...or at least the most televised year since I have been alive.

It's crazy. This was history in the making, and we are living proof. Take a moment to truly reflect. It will blow your mind…well, it blows mine.

"behind the badge"

"You have to look at this. This is bad." – 25-year-old middle eastern officer

I'll never forget this day. I was sitting in my patrol vehicle typing up a report from an arrest earlier that morning. It was February 23, 2020, when **Ahmaud Arbery**, an unarmed black man, was shot and killed while jogging through a neighborhood in Georgia. Two white residents of Glynn County, Georgia, chased and eventually shot and killed Arbery, stating they were trying to make a citizen's arrest.

You all know the story.

I received a text message from a guy from my squad. The text read, ***"You have to look at this. This is bad."*** Attached to the text message was a link to the video of the shooting.

Honestly, I was not sure what to expect. I opened the video and felt my mouth immediately drop. I began to get knots in my stomach, you know, the nervous feeling of anxiety when you're about to deliver a speech in front of hundreds of people, or I don't know, the nervous feeling you get when you are going into an interview for a position you really, really want.

Well, I watched the video two times, trying to figure out what happened. *Is this real? Where is this? What?*

A few minutes later, my team was called in to do extra patrol near our department headquarters. There was intel that there was going to be a protest and candlelight vigil for Ahmaud Arbery.

Before the candlelight vigil, we had a briefing. At this briefing, our field lieutenant shared with us the details of an incident in Georgia. We received information that there would be a protest demanding the arrest of the men responsible.

- *"Maybe he deserved it."*
- *"How is this our problem? We aren't even in Georgia."*
- *"They always want to protest about something."*
- *"Well, what did the guy do to get shot?"*

These were all comments made by officers from my department.

As the room fell silent, I wanted to speak up, *"Now is my time,"* I thought. Taking a deep breath, I froze, I literally froze. My body seemed to seize up, freezing in place as if time had come to a standstill. Angry, I desperately began searching for words to say, but it was like my mind was so clouded I couldn't make up a sentence.

I knew if I spoke, I would get emotional. You just watched the video, I thought. Oh my gosh, keep it together. I looked around the room and noticed I was the only black person. I told myself I was not strong enough. After seconds ticked by, it was time for our detail. I felt trapped. I was unable to break free from my fear of saying the wrong thing or being shut down. So, instead, **I said nothing**.

I stood and watched silently as I observed community members protest, demanding the arrest of the Arbery's murderers. The protest went by rather quickly; I'm almost positive I may have blacked out. My blackout was most certainly caused by my inability to see past my shortcomings and the constant stream of negative self-criticism of my failure to speak up. I was drowning in these thoughts, making it difficult to focus on anything else. **[Please do not do this. Be more forgiving of yourself. We all make mistakes.]**

Anyway. The protest was peaceful. I still feel a sense of guilt for not speaking up. *Why didn't I say anything?* It hit differently. I'll tell you one thing: this incident ignited something inside of me. From here on out, I refused to be silent. That was it. I am in this position for a reason. **YOU are in YOUR position for a reason.** Use your voice to stand up for what you believe in. While I am a police officer, I am also black. My blackness will ALWAYS show up first, with or without my uniform.

***Tip:** You are so strong! I hear you. I see you. Your emotions are valid. Your words are powerful.*

"behind the badge"

"Are you okay?" – 30-year-old female officer who happens to be black

R.I.P. GEORGE FLOYD

Nationwide Civil Unrest after the murder of GEORGE FLOYD

- *"He died because he was high."*
- *"It's not like he was an upstanding citizen"*
- *"He shouldn't have resisted."*
- *"He could breathe if he was talking."*
- *"People make him seem like he was an innocent man."*
- *"I hate when people try to bring race into it."*

The aforementioned comments were made in my presence, by police officers employed by my department.

Shocked? Probably not! I mean, I'll admit, I was pretty shocked. These were not the only comments being made. I just highlighted a few.

After not speaking up in the Ahmaud Arbery briefing, I tried my hardest to challenge comments made in my presence. I wanted to make them feel as uncomfortable as they made me feel every day. It was mentally exhausting.

Today, I cried. I cried before work. My thoughts began to race through my head. They were so intrusive I couldn't stop them. My heart began to pound rapidly in my chest, and it felt like an elephant was sitting on top of me as I began taking long, shallow breaths. I felt a lump in my throat…that lump you get when you know you are about to start crying.

Fun fact: the technical term for the "Lump in your throat" is Globus pharynges, which simply means that the lump sensation you feel is due to your muscles tightening up when sadness is being suppressed.

So, I cried today. I wanted to call in sick, but I rarely called off of work. I couldn't. Instead, I ugly cried in the shower. I didn't see how I looked, but I knew my face wasn't pleasant; I mean, I was in the shower sobbing. I was exhausted. I was angry. And I really didn't want to put on my police uniform today. I allowed myself the space to release my overwhelming emotions and feelings of helplessness. I cried.

After taking long, deep breaths to calm my nervous system, I found a quiet space in my apartment to chill and collect my thoughts before work. I had five hours before my shift. Five long, dreaded hours. I laid down on my carpeted living room floor and began to mindlessly scroll on Instagram. At this point, my phone was my companion. I reposted every George Floyd post.

After the fourth repost, a fellow co-worker DM'd me (also known as direct messages) on Instagram.

Her message read, ***"Are you okay?"*** I wanted to reply, *"No, I am not okay, dummy!"* Instead, I wrote, "I will be." She responded, "At least we weren't involved." I left the message on read.

Hmm. I don't know. As a black woman who is a black police officer, I feel somewhat helpless. Every story surrounding police brutality and/or violence publicly shared on news outlets and social media is triggering. *How does this not bother you?* I wondered. *Why are you not upset?*

I never really got along with this girl. I mean, after all, she was another black female officer, so in that sense, we had somewhat of a connection, something in common, right? We never hung out, though. I just acknowledged her in passing, like the simple, *"Hey girl,"* or *"Wassup?"* or *"How are you?"* Nothing more, nothing less.

At that moment, while lying on my apartment living room floor, it dawned on me. I now understood why, all these years, we never truly clicked. It was simple: she was no longer one of us. She was just black passing. She had fallen into the sunken place[8] y'all like LaKeith Stanfield in the movie *"Get Out by Jordan Peele"* only she never got out.

Ahhhhh! This explains her bizarre behavior and weird responses. She was in a tranced state of mind. Confused. Perhaps, even hypnotized. It was that cup of tea.
How must one escape the "Sunken Place?" Girl, wake up!

Nooooooo! Don't sink. Don't sink. Don't sink.
Welp, you know what they say, *"All skin folk ain't kin folk."* I get it now. I truly do. Do they still say that?

---

[8] The "Sunken Place" A disadvantaged person who is unwilling to see that they have been conditioned into acquiescence.

Tip: Don't allow yourself to fall into the "sunken place." You are too smart!

"melanin in the workspace"

"I can't watch NBA or NFL anymore because they're making it about politics. Have you seen their jerseys? They all have BLM phrases."- Group of white male officers and a grumpy sergeant.

What started as a nice, relaxing lunch quickly went sideways. Let me explain: 1) I hate eating lunch with co-workers who talk about politics, 2) Don't ask to see my lunch, and 3) Don't ask to try anything. Just eat your food, and I will eat mine.

Okay, I know it sounds a bit harsh, but those are my three rules. I deal with people every day and need some boundaries. I just wanted five minutes to myself. Is that too much to ask? Five minutes of silence. I was looking forward to a peaceful lunch, a break from my chauvinistic co-workers.

As I settled into the corner spot of the table, about to take my first bite of the mouthwatering spaghetti I made, I heard footsteps coming toward the lunch table. One by one, three to four of my co-workers began taking their seats at the table. So yeah, in a matter of moments, my joyous, well-deserved solitude was interrupted, and now we were having our lunch together.

I have been waiting all morning for an appropriate time to eat my spaghetti. I am not a breakfast person, so spaghetti was my first meal of the day. So you can understand my enthusiasm for it. It was really what I was looking forward to. We often eat lunch together as a squad…you know, for that camaraderie. If these co-workers were cool, I wouldn't have minded, but quite frankly, I hated eating with them. It's so incredibly awkward.

We have conversations about things I don't necessarily care about because our interests are different. It could also be because I am just checked out. I am exhausted and tired of all the subtle micro-aggressions and racism that surround me in my place of employment.

No matter how hard I tried to ignore their conversations, the voices around me grew louder and louder taking away my comfortable silence, making it difficult to focus on my own thoughts. The short experience of a relaxing lunch atmosphere transformed into a debate highlighting sports and politics. When I heard my co-worker say, "Kaepernick," my curiosity piqued. I lifted my head, opened my eyes a little wider, and looked toward him. I was now invested. *"What are they going to say next?"* My curiosity killed my indifferences.

My former partner confidently and pridefully said "I stopped watching the Super Bowl when Kaepernick started kneeling during the national anthem. That kid is a joke."

My grumpy sergeant followed the statement by saying, ***"I can't watch NBA or NFL anymore because they're making it about politics. Have you seen their jerseys? They all have BLM phrases."***

Mind you, this was the same grumpy sergeant who asked me why there was a need for a Black Police Officers Association when white people don't have any associations and went on to complain about celebrating Black History Month.

Back to the matter at hand, in unison, these detectives all seemed to be in agreement. Nodding their heads while they smacked on their unhealthy, greasy food. They were so proud they chose not to watch any televised sports. The conversation continued but now shifted to their disapproval of Lebron James because he, a black man, was using his platform to speak out against police brutality.

These guys are so lame, I thought.

Shut up! Shut up! Shut up! I just wanted to yell this at the top of my lungs. I didn't.

I simply retorted, "I love Lebron James."

Tip: Some people are just lame. Most would say if you can't beat them, join them. Don't join them... Do not!

exhale
the
ignorance

"melanin in the workspace"

"Why are you doing this? 30-year-old Black female co-worker. "I want to make them feel as uncomfortable as they have made me feel." -The elite passive aggressive person, aka me.

I am not saying this is right. I know you can't change the narrative of any situation, nor can you effect change without communication, but hear me out. Please?

Not all passive-aggressive behavior is aimed toward hurting someone. Although I don't think it's always a healthy or productive way to communicate, some things are better left unsaid. I like to think there is a time and a place for being passive-aggressive. **This was the time!**

After hearing the endless negativity toward black people, black history, black culture, and BLM, I had enough. During the month of February, I made a vow, to myself, of course, to wear some type of Black History Month shirt.

At this point in my career, I was a plainclothes detective. I did not wear suits unless I had to testify in court; jeans and a comfortable t-shirt was my uniform. Being on the narcotic street team granted me the ability to do the **black history month t-shirt challenge** because I was no longer required to wear a police uniform.

Bear with me now. I made this challenge up. Please feel free to join or start one at a police department near you.

The rules are simple. Wear any shirt that displays the faces or names of notable black figures in the fight for racial justice.

T-shirts can have slogans, graphics, or messages in support of black culture.

Although I had a few, I got the majority of my shirts on Amazon. Thank the Lord for the two-day shipping. I ordered a bunch of shirts with black educators, poets, artists, inventors, and rappers. I don't recollect how much I spent, but mind you, it was worth it all. It was worth the looks, worth the questions, and worth the stares from my co-workers. Worth every last penny! I even had a pair of socks with images of LA rappers (This was a gift).

During the second week, I explained the challenge to my co-worker. And awkwardly laughing, she asked, ***"Why are you doing this?"***

I exuberantly replied, ***"I want to make them feel as uncomfortable as they have made me…US…feel."***

With a smile from ear to ear, she appeared to be amused as she replied, "Ahhhh."

The next day, she wore a Malcom-X shirt☺.

Tip: *Always reward yourself for the small wins.*

"melanin in the workspace"

> ***"How can I be an ally as a white person?"*** *– my amazing partner, who happens to be white.*

"Buzz, Buzz, Buzz…" My phone was continuously going off. The only person who normally calls me right before work is my mom. She checks in on me almost every day. She's kind of like, obsessed with me. Haha! I'm playing. She just wants to make sure I am safe. I used to send a "C4[9]" every time I got home after an operation to put her at ease. She is such a sweetheart.

Well, it wasn't my mom. It was my partner. I felt myself let out a prolonged sigh, *"Ughhhh, are they calling us in early?"* I nervously picked up the phone, "Uhh, hello…" "Hey, do you have a minute," he asked. Uh-oh, normally, when people ask if you have a minute, it's something bad. "Sure, what's up?" I asked.

Before I go into the conversation, I just want to paint the picture for you. This man was, by far, hands down, my favorite person in the entire department, the entire department. We clicked. We vibed. We had each other's back. True partnership. He was a real one. As real as they come!

He asked, "How are you feeling with all this stuff going on? The protests. George Floyd. How are you?"

Honestly, before answering, I secretly smiled. *"Wow,"* I thought. He was a real friend, but I knew that. I

---

[9] Police terminology meaning "Clear" or "No further assistance needed."

mean, if I thought I was going to be asked this question by any officer or co-worker, I knew it would have been by him. Nonetheless, I wasn't expecting this conversation at all.

I answered, "Honestly, it's hard." He timidly said, "*I am not racist. I don't condone any of this behavior. I just want to know how can I be an ally as a white person?*"

I stuttered. I wasn't even ready to answer this question. Was it because I have never been asked this question or because I didn't plan on being asked this question in this conversation? Was I afraid of saying the wrong thing? So many emotions going through my head, too many to count.

I stumbled through my response but essentially said, *"I think the best way you can be an ally for me and other black and brown people is to take on the issue of racism and make it your own problem. While you'll never truly know how we feel, you have the ability to speak up in rooms where I do not. Educate yourself on the issues, listen, and speak up when something is not right because we…or I am counting on you. I can't do it alone."*

We ended the phone call shortly after. This is what an ally looks like. I told you all there are good officers, and he is living proof of that.

Just remember that when you group all officers together, it's like me saying, "All white people." It's not all white people, again somewhat anecdotal.

Tip: Get yourself some Allies! We can't do it alone. Challenge those conversations. Shift the narrative.

"melanin in the workspace"

"What do you think about BLM?" - 40-year-old white officer

Wait what…what do you mean, **what do I think about BLM?** I paused. Wondering, is this real? Is he really asking me how I feel about BLM? I smiled and replied, "Well…I'm black, and I do believe black lives matter." This was the perfect opportunity to ask him the same question.

I quickly added, "What do you think?" He answered, "Well, I believe all lives matter."

Ugh! The typical response from my fellow officer, of course. It was not a surprise that he would say that. Quite frankly, I was just so tired of arguing this notion. Exhausted. I responded, "Hmm," then tried to follow the unpleasant, annoyed, distasteful "Hmm" with the reason why I hate hearing people respond to black lives matter with All Lives Matter.

Black Lives Matter (BLM) is a social movement started in response to racism and violence against black people. I believe some of you have confidence in the idea that racism and violence against black people began in 2012 when Trayvon Martin was fatally shot to death while walking home after being reported to the police as "suspicious." No, we didn't forget.

Oh no, no, no, this BLM movement was started to address, highlight, educate, and shine a light on the years, and I mean YEARS, of racism. These racially charged incidents toward black people reignited the flame of anger about racism. This didn't just happen overnight, Silly.

Okay, I am not the type to go on and on about racism and all the racial injustices we, as black and brown people, face. This book isn't solely about the racism that exists. We all know it exists. This is about the *"All Lives Matter"* response I received from one of my white male co-workers.

I tried to explain it using plain English. I tried to break it down. Of course, I believe ALL LIVES MATTER; I believe ALL lives should be treated equally. However, I do not believe Black Lives Matter means the other lives don't matter. We are attempting to recognize and shed light on the fact that **Black Lives Matter, too.** When you say *All Lives Matter* in response to someone saying *Black Lives Matter*, for me, it feels like you are trying to derail, dismiss, and ignore the specific conversation about racism against black people.

When I was responding, I felt that damn lump in my throat. Ugh, I told myself, *"Don't start tearing up…hold it in."* Unfortunately, this is a common occurrence; I am outnumbered, but I still spoke my truth. I ended the conversation by saying Black Lives Matter is a declaration that black lives do matter, PERIOD.

Of course, after this conversation, it was a bit awkward for a few weeks. Many of my co-workers appeared to be walking on eggshells when speaking to me. Most didn't speak at all, just smiled or acknowledged me with a subtle head nod.

Fortunately for me, I had a safe space to retreat to. A space where I felt comfortable to share my frustrations, my fears, and my concerns. That safe space was my family group chat. I can always count on one of my siblings to send a meme to make me laugh. I can always count on my mom to send some words of encouragement.

Tip: BREATHE, just breathe, and hit up your support group, whomever it may be. You are not alone!

"melanin in the workspace"

"Thank you for sharing. I'm glad you took the time to put into words what most of us were thinking" – 45-year-old black male officer.

My Instagram Days, I used to be on Instagram all the time. Posting, reposting, commenting, and aimlessly scrolling. I must say, I became a great Instagram detective. I could find out things you were trying to hide, things that you would only share with your "close friends" on Instagram. But I have since retired. I'm off the grid! No more social media for me. I used to wake up to Instagram, like most people. No shade. I kind of think I have traits of an addictive personality. I mean, I would stay hyperconnected to my social media accounts. I don't think it was normal. So, I quit social media cold turkey.

No warnings. No prep. No nothing. Very abrupt ending to something that once brought me some comfort. And it was one of the best things I did that year.

Come what may, I'd like to think at this point, we are like global virtual pen pals/friends. One sided of course. I write. You read. Still, being open and sharing my stories opens up a door of vulnerability.

So, with that, I wanted to share something I wrote and posted on Instagram after sitting on a panel put on by African American law students.

It's only right I give you my true, raw feelings and emotions during the time of the 2020 civil unrest. All jokes aside.

And what better way to do that than to share this with you all.

In June of 2020, still triggered, I wrote and shared,

As a black officer, I hear you! I see you! I'm with you! I'm angry, disgusted, infuriated, embarrassed, and hurt! I'm embarrassed and disgusted by the behavior and actions of those officers. I'm outraged and repulsed by the behavior of ALL officers who played a role in the murder of George Floyd. I agree with you, racist, tyrannical officers do exist, but I promise you that there are officers who believe in justice.

While I am furious about the murder of George Floyd and the continued killings of our black and brown men and women, I do not agree with the violent stance being taken. I do not believe the behavior of the individuals who have turned to violence by throwing glass bottles, rocks, and bricks at us (police officers) should be defended or rationalized. I do not and will not ever condone the violent assaults on officers. Nevertheless, I understand where this pain and anger is stemming from.

WE ARE TIRED!

Despite the preconceived biases made when you see me in uniform, a black female police officer, I stand by George Floyd. I am against police brutality, and I'll be damned if I stop fighting this fight simply because I don't have the support of my black community or my law enforcement community. ***I will continue to fight this fight with you from the inside*** *by calling out racist officers or officers who use excessive force or even unnecessary force.* ***I will continue to fight this fight with you*** *by educating those who are culturally incompetent. I will continue to use my voice, my knowledge, and my experiences to have these conversations about anti-racism, regardless of how uncomfortable it may make them feel.*

It's more than an issue with police departments and racist officers. This is a systemic issue. There is an issue with our criminal justice system.

The point of these protests is to shed light on the racial injustices, to bring attention to the constant killings of our black men and women, and to make the majority in these positions of power feel uncomfortable. The point of these protests should be to take a stance for what we believe in. Enough is enough.

We need to influence public opinion and government policy. We need to educate ourselves on those policies. We need to know our local politician's policy on police brutality so that we are better equipped when we go to the polls. We need to do our research and then raise awareness. We need to vote!

Apply to become a member of the citizen review board on police practices in your city so that you have a say in reviewing and evaluating complaints against officers involving the use of force, criminal conduct, and discrimination. Attend your city council meetings. Apply to become a police officer to be a part of the change you wish to see. Shift the narrative. Yes, protests are powerful, and our voices are being heard, but what's next?

WE SHOULD BE PLOTTING OUR NEXT MOVE.

*I challenge police departments to continuously evaluate the officers going through the hiring process and the officers in your department. If there is an issue of racial injustice or excessive force, do not turn a blind eye; clean that sh*t up.*

I challenge the community to change your narrative because we aren't all bad. My main focus is to serve and protect the lives of the innocent, to be a positive role model for people of color, and to hold my fellow officers accountable by calling them out and intervening when the force used is excessive. We have an issue with systemic racism and white supremacy. The system was not built for people of color to thrive, which is why we need to continue to work together to enact change.

After this post, I received nothing but love. That wasn't what the post was for, but I appreciated the support. One of the comments that stuck with me was from a senior officer. He pulled me to the side that afternoon, raised his arm, wrapped it around my shoulder, you know, like a side hug, and said, ***"Thank you for sharing. I'm glad you took the time to put into words what most of us were thinking."***

I will never forget this moment. He was one of my mentors. This man introduced me to the hidden gem of working undercover, and let me tell you, working as an undercover officer has been one of the highlights of my career. When I tell you this man always looked out for me, he did, and for that, I will always be grateful. Needless to say, I appreciated hearing this from him. It truly warmed my heart.

Tip: Be intentional with your words. I challenge you to think about the words and messages you put out there.

<u>PART II:</u>

unapologetically FEMALE

"If they don't give you a seat at the table, bring a folding chair."- Congresswoman Shirley Chisholm.

(First black woman to be elected to the United States Congress)

Lanah Wright

unapologetically **FEMALE**

"black girl magic, literally"

Growing up, my mom always told me, *"You have to be twice as good as your male counterparts."* As a female working in a male-dominated position, you, like myself, are going to have situations where you may doubt your ability to perform up to the standards of your male coworkers. Not gon' lie, you will most likely get hit on by your coworkers and maybe even members of the community you took an oath to protect and serve. There will most definitely be some doubt by others in your ability to perform. They are a bunch of haters, for sure.

However, one thing to consider is that it will not last long, so stop whining. It's simple: do your job and prove those cynics wrong. That's it. I should probably make that a **TIP**, but I know you all are probably thinking, *"Tell us something we don't know."*

So let me just start by saying that while on duty, I got hit on A LOT! Okay, wait! I know my family likes to call me dramatic, but in this given situation, I am not being extra, and this is far from dramatic. You will see. I'm not egotistic or arrogant. So please do not get the wrong idea. I'd like to think I am a pretty humble person if I may say so myself, and no, I am not tooting my own horn, but *"beep-beep."* Okay…moving on.

I'm going to combine a few of the comments that I have received while on duty because if I don't combine them, I will keep repeating the same statements again and again and that will bore you to death. I'm sure you all can guess some of the comments made; I mean, sometimes men and women can be so predictable. Like, at least tell me something different. Spice it up if you're going to go out of your way to hit on me.

There were also incredibly inappropriate comments. I have decided to omit those because…eww yuck! So, as promised, here are a few of the many comments said to me while working on patrol….

1. *"Ooh, I'll let you lock me up any day."*
2. *"Are you married? If I was your husband, I would not let you work these streets."*
3. *"Can you have the female officer put me in handcuffs? She can handcuff me any day."*
4. *"Ooh, I love a female in uniform."*
5. *"You're too cute to be a cop."*
6. *"I want her to frisk me."*

Some men or boys would sing *"Mrs. Officer"* by Lil Wayne. It's actually funny because most of the time, they think they're being so original, but sorry your homeboy just sang the same song yesterday.

One male walked up to me and blatantly said, "I would f$%k the sh*t out of you if you let me."

Um, no, I will not let you. Sorry Mommy. Excuse my French. He said it, not me. Seriously though, definitely NOT attractive…weirdo. All of these comments came from men varying in age, all-wise and old enough to know it is not cool. It's just not. I'll give you my opinion on these comments. As annoying and even disrespectful as these comments will get, it's not the end of the world. Don't treat it as such.

While some of you agree with me, I know there are probably a few of you who may be thinking, *"Well, it's a compliment." Hmm, is it?* I have never taken these specific comments as compliments. Walking up to a woman and saying, *"You're really pretty or you are beautiful,"* aligns more with the true definition of a compliment. I feel like these comments play a huge role in the sexualization of the female with a badge, and as catchy as the song *"Mrs. Officer"* is, it does add to that narrative.

For those of you who won't publicly admit you do this, but know you have done this, STOP! It's neither cute, nor funny. And it's not attractive. It makes an already difficult job even harder. For those officers who just laugh when witnessing the blatant disrespect toward your female co-worker…

Grow up! It's not cute.

Tip: Your peace should be your main priority. Protect it at all costs.

"black girl magic, literally"

"*You're so fucking ugly; I would never date you*"- 35-40-year-old black male

This was my first year in the department. And for those of you who don't know, you are still considered a "boot.[10]" Basically, you're still a rookie cop. I successfully completed my four months of field training and was officially on my own, no longer a training unit. I loved it!

I had now experienced a bit of freedom. No one evaluating me, marking me down for my no good, sense of direction. Like, let's be real, they don't teach you north, south, east, or west in college. If you grew up in the 90s, you have never learned how to navigate to your next location by using a Thomas Guide, it's a map in a book. In the same way, we use Google Maps or Waze to get to our destination safely, they wanted me to use a Thomas Guide. That's wild. Like, are we out in the wilderness or something?

You don't learn that in high school. The one thing I remembered from elementary school was that stupid mnemonic, *"Never Eat Sour Watermelon...North East South West,"* this mnemonic was supposed to help me navigate my way to radio calls while in-field training. Nope! Absolutely not! Okay, so I struggled with directions. That was my weakness, but handling myself and holding my own was not.

---

[10] The term "boot" originated from the military, where recruits would wear brand new boots that were stiff and uncomfortable. A "boot" is basically a probationer.

Sadly, I have been in a few fights growing up. These physical altercations that I was involved in were an act of self-defense, given that I was young and naïve I feel like I got a pass.

Let me clarify. In high school, I had someone threaten to beat me up after school because they assumed I was talking about them at a football game. You know what they say about assumptions…I thought, *"Girl, nobody is worried about you."* It was a Friday night football game, so that fight was going to have to wait until Monday morning.

She waited.

I was more than ready. As soon I got home, I proudly told my mom I was probably going to get in a fight. Without giving too much information, my mom explained to me how fighting was not the answer *wink wink* and quickly followed that with, "Don't go to school starting fights, but if she hits you, you better make sure you beat her ass!"

I was amped up! Yasssssss! My mom never curses. Except the occasional *"sh*t"* when she stubs her toe on the corner of the wall or that time when she lost her balance and fell while roller skating through the park. You know? Those are the times that deserve one or two curse words.

Like I said, I have had my fair share of fights. I never said I won all of them, but between that and my morning ritual of Billy Banks *"Tae Bo"* sessions with my mom, I was ready.

So, reflecting back to that time this criminal tells me he would never date me. It was a slow day downtown. We saw this guy who we knew was wanted. There *were* *"B.O.L.O" (Be on the lookout)* flyers posted everywhere. He had an active felony warrant.

My partner and I saw this guy casually walking near our downtown train station. My partner conducted a records check, just to make sure the warrant was still active, while I continued to watch him. "Yup, the warrant was still active," he said. In full police uniform with markings and gear that clearly identified us as law enforcement officers, we hopped out of our marked patrol vehicle.

I don't know how officers reading this feel about my tactic, but as I walked toward him, I called his name, "Hey, John Doe." I did that to get his attention. Normally, if they don't know they have a warrant, they'll stay, but not this guy. He knew!

I watched as he slightly turned his head to look at me, not his full body, just his head. He made eye contact with me and began to shift his weight to his right side. With his eyes, he was looking to his left and right as if he were looking for an exit. I could feel it. He was about to run.

We continued to walk toward him. I started to skip a little bit, so I at least had a head start. You can't immediately start running toward them if they haven't started running. My philosophy is that if he wasn't planning to run and he saw officers running, he would now definitely start running. It's that simple. So, instead of a full run, I loudly said, "John Doe, we just want to talk to you."

He knew I was lying.

He dropped his bag and bolted. Full sprint. The shift from walking to his sprint was as if he heard a gunshot at a track meet. He switched gears and went into a full sprint. *Nooooooo! Are you serious?* After letting out a huge gasp, I whispered to myself, *"Here we go again."*

I watched as he ran into the train station, dodged a few people and benches, then exited through the back entrance. Ahhh bad move on his behalf, but a win for us. The exit didn't go through to the street so he was stuck. In other words, he was trapped. But that didn't stop him. He jumped onto the trolley tracks and continued running.

UGGGHHHH! Still running behind him, at last, I got within arm's reach of him. Once close enough to grab his arm, I loudly announced, "Police, stop running," as I simultaneously extended my left arm to grab his jacket to pull him closer to me or me closer to him. I thought this was a good idea. Thought.

He kept running, causing me to lose my balance, and that's what happened. I started to lose control, and I had no intention of letting go of the hold I had on him. At this point, he was basically dragging me.

This guy was not going to stop unless forcefully stopped and my body was slowly surrendering to gravity. My knees slowly get closer to the ground. I began using both arms to wrap around his ankles as I fell. Yup, I fell. Anyways.

I could feel my left knee scraping against the pavement through my uniform pants. The steady thumping of my heartbeat pumping adrenaline through my veins.

Wait, it was not over yet. I stayed on his ankles. Luckily, because of my defensive tactic training, my senses were sharp. I wrapped both arms around his ankles, which FINALLY caused him to fall. While on the ground, I heard loud stomps echoing on the pavement. My partner was close, and I could hear him yell, "Stop resisting," as he jumped in to assist. What felt like an eternity was less than a minute of a brief struggle. We successfully placed him in handcuffs and transferred him to jail.

Phew!!! So far, I have never lost a footie[11] I hate losing. I mean, I have been close, but as long as I am close

---

[11] Officer slang for a foot pursuit.

enough to put out the direction the suspect is running over the radio, I will never lose. Hopefully.

Oh, I forgot to mention he was about 6'3. As you can imagine, he had some difficulties sitting in the back of the patrol vehicle, as if those marked patrol vehicles weren't already uncomfortable.

Being the kind person that I am, I attempted to offer assistance, "Here, let me help you," he furiously replied, "Nah, b$t*h, you ripped my jacket." I looked at his jacket. It was indeed ripped.

Oops! I apologized. I mean, it was not intentional, but *"Why would you run?"* I thought to myself.

My partner and I escorted him to the booking processing area of the county jail. I instructed him to have a seat on the bench, to which he complied. As I began the paperwork, my partner stood by watching him.

While facing away from him, I felt a strange sensation, like that weird feeling when you know someone is staring at you. I turned my head to look in his direction and noticed him fixedly staring at me.

His stare was piercing, as if he was trying to kill me with his eyes. Despite the discomfort, I found myself staring back. I never lose a staring contest, so why start now?

As we were secretly competing to see who was going to look away first, he sucked his teeth, expressing disapproval, and said, ***"You're so fucking ugly, I would never date you."*** I smiled and asked, "You think I would date you?"

At that point, I knew I won...I mean, if it was a competition.

We successfully booked him into police custody. I never did see my future husband again.

Tip: Kill em with kindness. Always!

"I love a girl in uniform..."
"I want her to search me..."
"Women shouldn't be cops..."
"come put me in handcuffs..."
"Mrs. Officer, Mrs. Officer..."
"you're too pretty to be a cop..."
BLACK
OFFICER
"I would let you arrest me any day..."
"I would never let my girl be a cop..."
"Lock me up, baby..."

"black girl magic, literally"

"Can you discuss the internal battles that you feel/felt being a black woman as a police officer? How does it feel to put on that uniform every day? "- 26-year-old female law student

In the midst of George Floyd's murder, I was asked to be a panelist for a discussion surrounding race, policing, and racially motivated murder in America. Intense right? These topics certainly had the potential to ignite passionate debates and stir up deep emotions.

This panel was put on by the Student Bar Association and black law students. It was comprised of black law students, one retired black female police officer, a current black police officer, yours truly, of course, and black law professors.

I had never been on a panel in my role as a police officer so I was a bit hesitant to commit to sitting on this panel, but I was asked by my amazing sister, which meant I couldn't say no. Right?

As the day of the panel discussion approached, a mix of excitement and nervousness flowed through my body. Thoughts raced through my head...*Would I respond appropriately? Will I be considered a traitor to my black community? What would they think of my responses? Will I be called a traitor by my police community?*

I mean, the thought of speaking before a large audience of law professors and law students was intimidating, to say the least.

On the day of the panel, I received the following text message from my sister:

Hi Sissy! Reminder, the event starts in 15 minutes. I'm so proud of you!

I'm ready!!! What's the zoom info?

Ahhhh! I don't really think I was ready. My nervousness intensified. Well, it's here. Since the event was on Zoom, I was dressed in my "Sunday's Best" dress attire from the waist up. I didn't plan on standing up, so we were good.

I was let into the Zoom meeting ten minutes before the start time. Here we go! With a newfound resolve, I took a deep breath and smiled while turning my camera on. I secretly scrolled through the list of participants on the Zoom call. Wow! Already 40 people logged on. Everyone was on time…probably because they were law students.

We started with introductions and then dived straight into questions. Here are a few of the questions that were asked:

1. ***"What has been the most frustrating aspect of recent events, excluding the obvious trauma of Ahmaud Arbery, Breonna Taylor, and George Floyd's murders?"***
2. ***Have you ever felt/been ostracized by either the police community or the black community?***
3. ***Can you each discuss the internal battle that you feel/felt being a black woman as a police officer?***

As the discussion unfolded, my nervousness began to dissipate. I knew I was in a safe space. I found comfort in the shared vulnerability of my fellow panelists, especially my fellow officer. I admired her a lot. She was a black female officer who was making waves before I got on the department and has since retired. She spoke honestly and passionately about her experiences. She was the essence of black girl magic.

"Can you each describe your experience during the protests? How did/does it feel putting on that uniform every day?"

This is the question that got me.

My lips began to tremble a bit. I could feel it. As my eyes began to water, I fought hard to hold back my tears. While sitting at my kitchen table, I began to clench my fists underneath the table, trying to control the surge of emotions that began to overwhelm me. I felt that lump in my throat. I just knew I was about to start crying.

Maybe I can pull it together. *"I don't want to seem weak,"* I thought to myself. After a deep breath, I responded, *"Difficult."* All eyes were still looking at me; they were still waiting for a response from me, so I spoke honestly about my experience.

It was my first time speaking about my experience, the pain, frustration, and the internal battle I, like many black and brown officers, faced. We carry the weight of history, along with the weight of our own experiences. It is a constant battle. So yes, I was the emotional panelist, but I spoke from my heart. I wanted to give a voice to all those who felt like they could not share their experiences, I was once you.

Phewwwww! The panel was done. I survived. This was an amazing discussion put on by the Student Bar Association and black law students. Shout out to them! I truly believe this conversation needs to happen throughout colleges worldwide. It's necessary.

Shortly after the panel ended, I had to rush to work. I had this feeling of a weight lifted off my chest. A small sense of liberation that washed over me.

While driving I began replaying my answers and responses in my head. *Did I do well? Were they pleased with my responses?* In the midst of my overwhelming thoughts, I began receiving screenshots of text messages sent to my sister during and after the panel discussion.

Check it out.

I love you sister's heart. She is so pure and full of light and love.

This is so powerful.

Love her. Tell her that I love her and sending her hugs & thank you for sharing

chills

Sissy: RIGHT!!

Wow her story was so powerful and I'm glad she shared it

Your sister was amazing #blackgirlmagic 🖤

Sissy: Man, she has me crying omg lol I just wanna hug her

LOVE THIS SO MUCH

Tip: *A lil' reminder for you: Don't be afraid to sprinkle your magic, everywhere. We see you, and they will listen.*

"black girl magic, literally"

"It's okay. Most women have a difficult time. You guys aren't meant to shoot a shotgun. It's just your anatomy" –
White male sergeant

I failed the shotgun qualification shoot. I have never shot a shotgun in my life, let alone any firearm, so this was definitely a learning curve for me. I did well with my pistol shooting, but struggled with the shotgun. If you have ever shot a shotgun before, you and I both know the kickback, also known as the recoil[12], on the gun, is insane.

After the failure, I was overwhelmed with emotions. It wasn't just failing the shotgun qualification shoot, I felt like I failed to meet my goals and aspirations of becoming a police officer. I invested so much time and effort into pursuing this career. I was embarrassed.

Prior to the police academy, I would wake up and train with my dad at 5:00 a.m., running five miles without music or gum, just my thoughts. Insane right? With every stride, the sound of my shoes hitting the pavement created a steady cadence. A sound you begin to appreciate. My dad, of course, still had his headphones in, blasting worship music the entire way. Lucky.

In the evenings, my mom would take me to local fast-food restaurants that had six-foot walls. When I discovered I had to be able to hop over a six-foot wall during the police physical assessment test, she was on it. We trained…well, I

––––––––––––––––––––

[12] The backward force that a shooter experiences when firing a shotgun or gun.

trained to get over the six-foot walls, my mom watched and believed she gave me tips.

I mean, of course, there was some external pressure, but I attributed my sadness to my personal disappointment. As you can see, I worked extremely hard.

After failing, one of the police sergeants at the academy walked me to my car and said, ***"It's okay. Most women have a difficult time. You guys aren't meant to shoot a shotgun. It's just your anatomy.***" Not knowing if that was supposed to be comforting or a subtle jab, I softly replied, "Yeah." I would've taken the good ole' *"Don't worry, you'll get it next time"* or *"Don't give up. You got this."* Sadly, this sergeant was not capable of being sensitive.

I went home and started applying for teaching jobs. My negative thoughts were chipping away at my self-esteem. I know it sounds a bit melodramatic, but I really did find myself questioning my ability to be an officer. Well, *"maybe this position was not in God's plan,"* I thought. All the naysayers were right.

While applying for different jobs, something safe, I called my mom, crying. Her advice, which is something I would like to share with you all, was this; ***"Move away from the negative thinking…that's faulty thinking.***" So, you do just that in whatever trial you're going through.

Sit in your emotions! Through the years, I have learned that it is okay to be disappointed. Just don't let that disappointment take over. Always, always, always trust in your abilities. I know it is easier said than done, trust me. **I had to continue to trust God** and encourage myself, even in my time of defeat. Remember that all things will work together for your good. Can I get an Amen? No seriously….

Anyways, years later, I ended up becoming an expert shotgun shooter. I now love shooting a shotgun, the only issue I have is the amount of rounds it holds.

***Tip:** Trust yourself! I believe in you. Your thoughts really do produce actions that tend to echo out into eternity.*

Water You
be your own cheerleader
encourage yourself

"it's a ~~boy~~ girl thang"

*"**Well, more than half of the applicants, especially women, have a difficult time with some of the questions asked. You can try to reapply in a year**"* – Male police recruiter.

When I was first applying to become a police officer I applied in an extremely Caucasian area. If hired, I would've been the only sworn black female officer. I believe there were about 40 sworn police officers in their department.

On interview day, I arrived dressed in my finest pants suit. I was told as a woman applying for a police officer position, I should avoid wearing a skirt and a blazer because it would bring too much attention to my legs, so instead I wore a cute, fitted suit and some heels. When I entered the building I was greeted by the receptionist who instructed me to have a seat. A few minutes later, I heard, "Ms. Wright," a male voice called from inside the interview room. It's game time, I thought.

The interview started off smoothly. I was asked typical interview questions, along with a few scenario-based questions. Just when things were going well, the interview quickly took a left when I was asked, *"Could you ever shoot and kill someone?"* As I squinted my eyes and slightly tilted my head in confusion, I stumbled through my response, "No." I know, I stumbled through a two-letter word…pathetic. My mind went blank. I couldn't seem to come up with a coherent response. At the time, I honestly couldn't imagine shooting and killing someone. **Could you?**

After the interview, I spoke with my friend's mom, a well-respected black female detective, and told her the question and answer. She listened and put it into perspective for me. After speaking with her, I thought, sure, if the suspect was putting a civilian, myself, or my co-worker's life in danger, and it was a question of whether or not any of us would leave the incident alive, I would always choose the latter. However, that was not the question asked.

One week later, I got a call from the recruiter saying I failed the oral examination. When I asked why, he unashamedly said, ***"Well, more than half of the applicants, especially women, have a difficult time with some of the questions asked. However, you can reapply in a year."*** Really? I figured most human beings may have a difficult time with some of the questions asked, not just women. I responded in my head; I couldn't share my true feelings. Instead, I replied, "Okay."

Well, I failed that portion and never looked back. I went on to apply to a few different agencies and used that interview as training and preparation.

***Tip:** Don't ever forget what God has for you no man can take from you. It was simply not meant to be. I did not give up, and neither should you.*

"it's a ~~boy~~ girl thang"

"I can't justify sending two people to the training" – white police sergeant.

I had difficulty figuring out where this incident should have been placed in this book. I wasn't sure if I should put it under unapologetically BLACK or unapologetically FEMALE. I could not definitively say I was treated this way because I was the only female on the squad. It also crossed my mind that it could be because I was the only black person on the squad. Either way, I thought it would be beneficial to share, so that's why I am sharing it with y'all.

It was a Friday, and this situation happened around 6:00 a.m. This was hearsay, but from a credible source. Let's rewind. On Thursday, I was helping a co-worker answer some follow-up questions for a narcotics operation we were working on. Everyone on my team knew of my interest in working with the Narcotics Street Team. I had worked as an undercover officer on several different occasions and had assisted them with multiple narcotics operations.

That Thursday, my co-worker and I expressed interest in attending undercover training. Although I had already operated in an undercover capacity, having the training to list on my resume looked even better. On behalf of myself and my co-worker, I notified my supervisor of the training and volunteered to email the sergeant in the Narcotics unit. My goal was to set up some undercover training for my squad. This was definitely doable and nowhere near an extreme, unreasonable request.

After working a 12-hour shift, working for a sergeant who constantly ignored me, avoided making eye contact with me, and only spoke to the men like we were in the 1800s, I left work to unwind, and of course have a glass of wine.

The following day, on Friday, around 6:00 a.m., I received a call from my co-worker. He started the conversation with, "Okay, so I don't know what good this is going to do by me telling you, but I thought I should let you know." At that moment, I knew the next thing he said was going to be something that annoyed me. I am actually a *"cool, calm, and collected"* person, but I, like most people, don't like to be played or disrespected.

Anyway.

As the conversation continued, he began telling me that our sergeant informed him that the Narcotics unit was putting on an undercover training for officers. My sergeant asked if my co-worker wanted to attend the training, to which he quickly said yes. After thanking my sergeant for the opportunity, my co-worker asked, "Hey, sarge, I know Lanah has expressed interest in working with the Narcotics unit. I know she would also be interested in taking this class." According to my co-worker, my sergeant, while walking away from him, casually replied, ***"I can't justify sending two people. She will probably not work narcotics, but you have a chance."***

Annoyed, I responded, "He can't send two people? He just sent two people to a leadership conference about a week ago!!!!"

About a week ago…*hits Bobby Shmurda's *"Shmoney dance"* as I revisit this moment in my book. Just kidding*

Okay, let's be serious. Correct me if I am wrong, were his actions not deliberate? As I continued to express my concerns about my sergeant's response to my co-worker, my annoyance grew. *"He does not like me, and that's okay,"* I thought.

On our first day back to work, acting oblivious, I walked up to my sergeant after line-up and asked, "Hey, Sarge, did I get approved for the narcotics training?" Knowing the answer, I felt a mix of curiosity and anticipation. There was a sense of excitement, wondering what response I was going to receive, knowing the answer.

My sergeant quickly replied, "Unfortunately not. They only wanted to send one officer." Liaaarrrrr! I wanted to yell at the top of my lungs, but instead replied, "Oh okay, maybe next time."

Four months later, I received a call from a Lieutenant in the Narcotics unit who asked if I was interested in working in that unit. I did not have to put in for the position, but was hand-selected without that stupid training. Look at God!

***Tip:** Life is 10% of what happens to you and 90% of how you react to it, especially in the professional world, which is full of politics. You don't want to burn any bridges. Keep your head up!*

"it's a ~~boy~~ girl thang"

***Cackling while yelling, "You think you're stronger than me. I'd like to see you try to put the cuffs on."*- Intoxicated 25–30-year-old white male**

He ferociously yelled this as he tried to spit in my face while I tried to place him in handcuffs. So disrespectful and disgusting. Working downtown, in my city's premiere entertainment district, we usually experience a humungous amount of intoxicated people. It wasn't a surprise for us. There are some who can take care of themselves and then there are those who are unable to care for themselves. He clearly could not handle his liquor.

This intoxicated male was jumping over the exterior patio gates of busy bars, which was not only disrupting the patrons inside, but also causing issues with the staff. I'm sure the security of the last bar asked this guy to leave their establishment before calling the police.

Once we were called, I noticed the male was sitting on the metal exterior patio gate. As my partner and I walked toward the male, I saw the security try to discreetly point at the male as if we didn't know who the culprit was. I mean, it was pretty obvious, given that everyone else was inside the bar having the time of their lives while this guy was surrounded by staff and security.

As we got closer, I noticed he wasn't a scrawny white male, he was buff. Every inch of his being exuded strength. His bulging muscles and chiseled physique were the epitome of physical strength. Clearly stronger than me and my squad put together, or so some thought. When he shouted, I could see his neck veins popping out. When he laughed, I could see his veins popping out. No! That is not normal. It can't be. He was intimidating for sure.

We all know alcohol affects individuals differently. This guy wasn't the fun, flirty, sad, or philosophical drunk. To our bad luck, this guy was a hostile, angry drunk. Ahhhhhhh! He was …the hulk! Just kidding. He had bushy eyebrows and a steely gaze. His glossy eyes felt like they were piercing my soul. I knew he was not going to go down without a fight. However, as daunting as he was, I knew with the right technique, if he didn't comply, I could take him.

My first approach is to kill em' with kindness. I tried the good ole verbal judo[13]. That did not work.

"Whaaaaa, whaaa offi…policeeee offisiirr, I did nothinggg." The odor of alcohol was unapologetically emanating from his breath, Yuck! It just hit me. I calmly said, "Sir, I can tell you've had a little too much to drink. I don't believe you are able to care for yourself, so I'm going to take you to a sobering center. Do me a favor and place your hands behind your back."

He smirked and replied, "No," while simultaneously grabbing the exterior metal patio gate. During the majority of my interactions, when I have the luxury of having a few minutes to think, I like to remind myself of the **ask, tell, make** rule. These are my rules. The rules that were taught to me in the police academy. It is somewhat of a step-by-step process or maybe similar to a process of elimination. Here is an example: I'm going to **ask** you once, maybe twice, then I will **tell** you. At this point, you have had <u>three</u> opportunities to comply. Unless there is a language barrier or a disability

---

[13] A technique that utilizes words to deescalate tense situations and communicate more effectively.

that prevents you from following instructions, the aforementioned task should have been completed.

"You're under arrest for being drunk in public, so let go of the gate and place your hands behind your back." At this point, we are in phase two…the **"tell"** portion of the rule.

He grinned and stood next to the exterior gate, passively resistant and uncompliant. So, I told him a second time to place his hands behind his back.

While holding on to the metal exterior gate, he turned his head toward me and looked at me with this piercing stare as if he was trying to intimidate or scare me. While staring, he cackled and said, ***"You think you're stronger than me. I'd like to see you try to put the cuffs on."***

We have now escalated to phase three, the *"***make***"* portion of the rule. My partner, standing on the other side of me, shouted, "Dude, let go of the gate and put your hands behind your back." "Haha," he laughed in response. I attempted to grab his right arm with both my right and left hand as he continued to hold on to the metal exterior gate.

Unfortunately, my physical strength alone was not helpful. With no choice left, I transitioned to pain compliance techniques. Without giving you our tactics, I'll say that these techniques involve activating pressure on areas that will create a sufficient amount of pain to achieve compliance. Now that worked.

Anyway, it took three officers to get this guy in custody, but we did it safely. He was later transported to the sobering center, where he remained for being drunk in public.

*Tip: **Technique** always wins, TRUST!*

"it's a ~~boy~~ girl thang"

"When I was looking for people that applied for this position, I caught myself thinking…well, how would the dynamic be if I added a female to the team? Then I stopped myself and said, well, why wouldn't I hire a female if she is the most qualified?" – my white male police sergeant of two years.

It's interview day. I felt a surge of confidence. I prepared for this moment…for this interview. Okay, typically, I am not the type to sit and talk about myself. I kind of hate it actually, but I prepared for this, and I was ready to showcase my qualifications. To be honest, I was not going to apply for this position, but was encouraged to do so by a few sergeants in my division. It was for a proactive unit in the police department, a well sought out spot.

Let me give you a little background: this team worked primarily in the city's downtown entertainment district. This team actively investigated alcohol, gang, and narcotic-related crimes…Exciting right? So, with all of my years of experience, I felt prepared. It was interview day, and I was convinced that this job was mine for the taking.

During the interview, I felt confident, however I do believe that some of my answers to their scenario-based questions may have been subjective. Even so, I noticed the main interviewer seemed pleased with my responses, based on the look on his face. Still, there was this bizarre, uncomfortable feeling of doubt that lingered in the back of my mind.

Finally, we reached the last few minutes of the interview. The nervousness began to flow through my body.

In an attempt to steady myself, I took a deep breath before I answered the last question. Although doubt crept in, making me question my ability to perform, I killed the last answer. I did! Like I said, I was prepared.

After the interview, I was eagerly awaiting the call inviting me to join the team. However, days turned to weeks and during the wait, an email announcement highlighting the opening of one position on the same team came out. Hmmmm? Maybe they are trying to hire an additional officer for this team. I was kind of frustrated, *"I mean, at this point, just give me an answer,"* I thought.

A month passed and no call. Crazy. That same day, I ran into the sergeant who conducted the interviews. I smiled and asked, "Have you filled the spot?" He quickly answered, "We have one more interview."

The next day I got a call. After spending weeks replaying my answers in my head, I finally got the call. I was offered the position. I was even given a start date. I thanked the sergeant for giving me the opportunity to join his team. Before ending the phone conversation, he followed his offer with, ***"When I was looking for people that applied for this position, I caught myself thinking…well, how would the dynamic be if I added a female to the team? Then I stopped myself and said, well, why wouldn't I hire a female if she is the most qualified?"***

Surprised, I simply replied, "Thank you."

Despite the glaring gender bias throughout local police departments, I think this story alone highlights the frequency with which we, as women, experience situations like this in our workplace. Unfortunately, I am not the only woman who has experienced this, AND this is not the only field where this type of discrimination occurs. As Big Sean rapped, *"That's not just the ~~NFL~~ (policing)...that's every field"* ("Thank You" by DJ Khaled ft. Big Sean). Okay, completely different context, but I think that line can be applied to different situations and still hold the same meaning. We gon' make it work.

Anyway. I told you all I was the most qualified. I am not an arrogant person, but the facts are the facts. We are conditioned, as black women, to dim our light so that they are comfortable.

Nah, STOP THAT!

***Tip:** Put yourself in a position where you are not twice as good, but 3x better.*
Be legendary.

"man-terruption**"**

"Blah blah blah," – a white 26-year-old male officer talking over me.

I found that in this career, most of the time if I respond to a scene with my male partner(s), people tend to direct their attention toward them. It's almost like they feel more at ease in the presence of a male police officer. Sometimes, during interviews or witness statements, I'd ask a question and already know that the answer would be directed to my male partner instead of me, the person who asked the question. Bizarre. I have also had some partners who attempt to take over the conversation by talking over me while I am still talking.

If you are a male officer reading this…**STOP DOING THAT!** If you are a male professional reading this…**STOP DOING THAT!** If you are a male reading this…**STOP DOING THAT!** We **[Women]** can speak for ourselves, thank you!

I like to call this trait the "Look at me, I am your male savior" trait, commonly referred to as male-dominant behavior. It's the idea that YOU, as men can interrupt, dismiss, or overshadow women in conversations they are having, ultimately undermining their contributions and perspectives.

Sadly, I see this happening far too often. What is the main reason men talk over women? I often ask myself. Power? Control? Who knows!

On this day, I was determined to passively address the issue when this occurred. I just kept talking. We were talking at the same time. So dumb, I know. I wanted to prove a point. I didn't do this while taking a statement or anything that would go on an official document. It was while talking to a citizen who explained to my partner and me that someone had stolen his property when he was sleeping in his tent.

Anyway, my partner stopped talking, and the male who was informing us of his stolen property began looking at me while I was speaking.

It worked!

Tip: My advice is to keep talking. Just keep talking, they will eventually get the hint. Petty, I know.

"breaking barriers"

"I was always told I could not be a police officer because I was such a small female. One day, you and your partner responded to a 911 call, and I saw you handling business. It was that moment I told myself, if she could do it, I can too." – Newer white female officer.

Growing up, I never personally encountered a black female police officer. I knew that the representation was starkly limited. I mean, of course, they were out there, but fate never gave me the opportunity to encounter any black women in law enforcement, well, until high school. My friend's mother was a detective for a local police department. I was surprised, but I wasn't shocked enough to want to pursue a career in law enforcement, it was just something I had never seen.

After graduating high school, I applied to a 4-year university, not truly knowing what I wanted to do with my life. Nine-year-old me wanted to be an actress, doctor, dancer, singer, **AND** lawyer…living in Hawaii…<u>Kauai, HI,</u> to be exact. My mom saved a lot of my childhood projects, which is why I can confidently share my nine-year-old aspirations with you. I was ambitious, to say the least. Take a look.

At age 11, I wrote the following in my journal, *"My favorite author is Robert Louis Stevenson. I enjoy drawing, playing the piano, and **writing stories about things that happen in real life. <u>I want to write a book one day.</u>"** Hold up…can we say full circle moment?

As I started writing this book, I didn't even remember dreaming of becoming an author. Shout out to my mom for saving some important stuff, along with all the non-important junk. Just kidding!

Well, at least I am on track to accomplish <u>**one**</u> of my **six** career goals in life. Haha! I guess you can say I tried the singing thing. Volunteering for all the solos at church, but I mean for those who know the story…well, let's just say I wasn't blessed with a voice like Whitney Houston, Beyonce, or Mariah Carey.

Going so completely off track from my childhood dreams, I first decided to pursue a career in sociology. My classes were okay, but after reading *"A Child Called It"* by Dave Pelzer, I changed my mind. This book didn't motivate me to become a social worker. It actually just highlighted situations I did not feel I would ever be equipped to handle. To all the social workers and people who work in the foster care system, thank you. Not everyone can handle what you all see every day.

In navigating my next steps in life and trying to get through the frightening, terrifying process of changing my major, I found myself bored flipping through television channels one day. I probably could've been doing some homework, but I was a procrastinator in college…I mean, maybe I still am, but that is not the point. Plus, I wrote my best papers under pressure.

Anyway. I stumbled across the show *"Law & Order: Special Victims Unit."* A fictional character, Detective

Olivia Benson, was on television investigating sex crimes. I honestly think the time I was watching this series she was the only female at the precinct, surrounded by men.

With every episode, I became more captivated by the cases she was working on. I found myself considering changing my major to Criminal Justice. I planned on investigating domestic sex trafficking cases.

Shortly after having this epiphany, I began thinking about my experiences with law enforcement. While my interactions were limited, I vividly remembered each one. You know what they say, *"People will always remember how you made them feel…"* or something like that. I know I am missing a piece of this quote, but you all get the point.

As you all read in the first chapter, I, too, have experienced a few things that warranted me calling the police. That experience was my first time reporting a crime. I anxiously awaited their arrival. While waiting, I began to second-guess myself, questioning if I had done the right thing. The uncertainty and fear lingered.

The arrival of the police did not instill a sense of security, the safety that is experienced by some, maybe most of my white classmates. I spent 15 minutes with them, and not once did either officer pull out a pen to write. I mean, memorizing a statement is crazy. I felt unheard and unsupported. The male officers were very dismissive and appeared to be disinterested. They offered no guidance or solutions and treated me, a victim, like a suspect.

"This is the last time I will ever call you guys," I apprehensively said. I even went on to tweet about my interaction with the officers, including their badge numbers and department they worked for. That was short-lived. My mom demanded I remove the tweet I was so proud of. "Mom, they didn't even care about anything I was saying. It was a joke to them and I want everyone to know. They acted like I was lying." Even though I was grown, a sophomore in college, I was still low-key afraid of disappointing my parents; I had to obey my mom, so I removed it.

Feeling helpless, my frustration only continued to grow with each day that passed. My last piece of faith in the criminal justice system faded and then out of nowhere…**booom, a crazy thought, a sudden revelation**. I began to develop a strong desire to become a police officer.

I am certain it was God! He wanted me there, in that position. I felt it. I found my purpose for that season of my life. I was reminded of how I was viewed as the suspect when reporting a crime and when stopped by the police in the pouring rain was treated with so much disrespect. Years later, I still remember the smirk on the officer's face when they were taking my statement. The undoubtedly negative experiences with officers served as a catalyst for change, and I was, in fact, going to be the change. I was determined to be.

I constantly reminded myself of those officers and thought I could do it better, way better. I will effect change from the inside. It was at this moment that I decided to pursue a career in law enforcement.

When the female officer shared she was *"…always told she couldn't be a police officer because she was such a small female,"* I looked at her and said, "Don't ever count yourself out. Don't let them tell you where you do and don't belong. You belong here. We need you." When I looked at her, I saw myself.

We exchanged smiles and left our separate ways.

*Tip: Whether you're a woman in law enforcement, a woman in the medical field, a woman in the entertainment industry, a woman in law, **heck, a woman in this world**, let us lift one another up. We need each other.*

<u>PART III:</u>

unapologetically POLICE

"Blessed are the peacemakers, for they shall be called the children of God" Matthew 5:9

unapologetically POLICE

As I was beginning to write this chapter, I wondered about all the content I wanted to include. In the process of inclusion and exclusion, I got the strong feeling that this chapter was going to be a hard one to write.

In the past few years, I've lost one of my closest friends, chose to love a few family members from a distance, and have ended dating relationships, not because of infidelity, not because of reoccurring issues throughout those relationships, but solely because I chose to be a police officer. The moment I put on that uniform I knew that I was now a part of one of the most hated, yet needed groups in the country. What a conundrum!

I found that because my career goals and dreams did not align with the plan that **others** had for me, I was wrong. ***Now read that again…***Does that make sense? **MY career** and **MY dreams** did not align with what **OTHERS** wanted me to do, which made me a bad person. Yup, you're reading that correctly.

For some, a person of color, a black, African American female or male, should not pursue a career in law enforcement because let's face it…police don't like black people. For those reasons, I have spent numerous hours trying to change the perspective of some of my closest friends, family members, my community, and the general public.

Well, I'm done.

I know my influence starts with me, no matter how small it may be. As a black woman, I will not compromise my convictions and my beliefs because I am a police officer.

On most days, I proudly wore my uniform, because I believed I was a small representation of people who look like me in this field. Let's be real: at times, just being a BLACK,

FEMALE (or MALE) **POLICE OFFICER** is a taxing assignment.

For me, there were days, many days, when I wanted to just give up. I'm sure you all have experienced this feeling at least once in your lifetime, and if you say you have not you are probably lying. No, I'm joking. If you haven't, well, I envy you.

Let's get into it….

I am currently sitting on my couch with a cup of black coffee. No sweetener, no milk added. I'm trying to be healthy. I have the television turned on, just for background noise, I guess. I wanted to start this chapter a little differently. I decided to start it with a written monologue from a well-known "cop" movie set in Los Angeles…END OF WATCH.

Being an officer, I can say firsthand that this movie does not accurately depict law enforcement…at all. Maybe back in the day, maybe in areas with more police corruption, but I decided to reference this movie because there are parts that hit home for me and probably many other officers. However, I won't speak for other people, but I am assuming that is why it's a fan favorite. I really shouldn't assume that, either. Anyway, here is the monologue.

Fun fact: The writer of Training Day, David Ayer, also wrote End of Watch*

Alright, back to the piece from End of Watch:

"I'm the police, and I'm here to arrest you. You've broken the law. I did not write the law. I may even disagree with the law, but I will enforce it, and no matter how you plead, cajole, beg, or attempt to stir my sympathies, nothing you do will stop me from placing you in a steel cage with grey bars. If you run away, I will chase you. If you fight me, I will fight back. If you shoot at me, I will shoot back. By law, I am unable to walk away. I am a consequence. I am the unpaid bill. I am fate with a badge and a gun.

Behind my badge is a heart like yours. I bleed. I think. I love, and yes, I can be killed, and although I am but one ~~man~~-person, I have thousands of brothers and sisters who are the same as me. They will lay down their lives for me, and I them.

We stand watch together, a thin blue line protecting the prey from the predators, the good from the bad. We are the police." *–Officer Taylor, End of Watch, 2012*

This quote hit home for me. I just felt this with all my heart. So much truth in my beliefs as an officer. So re-read if you need to, take your time, and process the statement.

"day one"

"First and last name, educational background, and why you chose law enforcement" – a 40-year-old academy training officer.

Like most jobs, in the interview room, you are normally asked why you want to be a… **[Insert YOUR Job Title.]** The same thing applies in the police academy; however, you have to share your answer with your academy mates and future co-workers. I think this is way more stressful than sharing it with a few panelists.

On **day 1** of the academy, our training officer stood in front of the classroom and said, "Tomorrow, each of you will arrive in suits for the first half of the day. You will each go around the room and introduce yourself by stating your *First and last name, educational background, and why you chose law enforcement.* It's simple, and you have the entire night to prepare, so I expect your speech to be flawless." While standing at attention[14], together we yelled, "Yes sir!"

I remember this day like it was yesterday. In an academy of 50 men and women, I was one of three black women. Little did I know, that was pretty good.

So, back to introductions, some of my white academy mates stated they came from a law enforcement family and always knew they wanted to be a cop. Even more of my

---

[14] A military posture where one quietly stands, with feet together and both arms at the sides. The body should be straight and stiff. No buckled knees.

white academy mates said they wanted to create change and serve their community.

After sitting through a few speeches, it was my turn. In my opinion, group-setting introductions are always awkward. We are no longer in middle school or high school, so why do I have to stand up in front of what felt like a room of students? I mean, I did it, but why?

Feeling extremely nervous, in a moment of panic, I swallowed my gum. Ugh, the minty flavor caused this uncomfortable burning sensation on the way down. It was a split-second decision, but I didn't want to chew gum while talking as it was too much of a distraction. I took a deep breath, faked my confidence, stood up, and essentially said, "My name is Lanah Wright. Unlike most, I never grew up wanting to be a cop, and I did not come from a law enforcement or military family. However, I have worked in a prison where I had the opportunity to teach inmates…who, just like us, are human beings. I have a substantial amount of education in the criminal justice field. I have watched people that look like me get targeted and have complained to my peers about it. This is my chance to make a difference."

Done. I spoke so quickly. It was like I blacked out. This was the start of my new season. I was nervous, but ready.

Although I adlibbed the first part after hearing that the majority of the police recruits came from a law enforcement or military background, I wrote the remainder of the speech the night before. In preparation, I practiced my speech a few times in the mirror. In that time, I learned three things about myself, I talk with my hands, my mouth moves in a weird way when I talk, and my right eye is smaller than my left, which is extremely noticeable when you have big eyes. Either way, I finished.

Here we are. Six years later. I am now one of seven black female officers in a department of approximately 1800 sworn police officers. I know every black female officer in the department; I am close friends with a few of them. We stick together because let's face it, we are all we have!

As a police officer, you're going to go through and be a witness to some crazy stuff, some funny stuff, and some really hard, sad stuff. I was always told you need to learn how to turn it off if you want to survive this career, which meant trying very, very hard to leave work…at work.

In this upcoming chapter, I will share a few stories of the many experiences I have had while being employed as a police officer. The exciting thing about this career is every day is different.

"10-8"

"Wait, did I step in dog poop?" – concerned police officer aka ME.

The area I patrolled was busy. Busy with urgent police radio calls, violent radio calls, non-emergency radio calls, and report-type calls, which are calls people make when there is no crime in progress, but individuals want to file a police report (i.e., burglary reports; theft reports; incident only reports). Oh, there were also the bogus, waste-of-your-time radio calls. Once these calls were on the board, we, the patrol officers needed to clear them.

While working patrol, one of our solo "John" [15] units responded to a disturbance call that had been holding for over three hours. The call was regarding a white female who had been seen yelling and throwing food at cars while standing at a busy intersection downtown. As soon as we cleared our officer lineup, this officer acknowledged the call and calmly said, "You can show me enroute to the disturbance call" over our police radio.

This was frowned upon and flat-out selfish. Since Mr. Eager Beaver volunteered for the call at the start of our shift, it limited the time we had to load up our gear, put fuel in our vehicles, and ease into a 10-hour shift.

He was solo, so one of us needed to cover him. Normally, it would be easier if another solo "John" unit covered him, so they aren't taking a two-officer unit out of the field. Of course, no one volunteered because this officer

---

[15] Single patrol officer unit

was somewhat of a…hmm…hot mess. Nice guy, a terrible, terrible officer. Anyway, my partner and I ended up covering this officer, so he wasn't handling the call by himself. Strength in numbers, Right?

Well, as we drove up to the incident location, I noticed the officer was already on scene talking to a white male. This was not the female that was seen causing the initial disturbance.

From a distance, I noticed the male had his hands deep inside his jeans pants pocket. This officer didn't care, but if I am going to stand and witness this conversation or "cover you," I'm going to need to do it safely. As I got closer, I politely asked, "Excuse me, sir, would you mind taking your hands out of your pocket while this officer is talking to you?" After a few jumbled, incoherent statements, I managed to make out a raspy "eeefffff youuuu!"

Okay, definitely not what I expected the first interaction of my shift to be like. I looked at my partner and the other officer in disbelief, wondering why we were still talking to this male, who was not even the subject of the radio call. The officer continued talking **nonsense** while instructing the male to pack up his tent. The male, who seemed visibly upset, began looking to the sky as if he was processing the officer's request to remove the tent.

I know you all are familiar with the potential dangers of the unknown, his hands in his pocket giving off the impression that there might be something he was hiding. I am not sure if it was a weapon, drugs, or just my paranoia, but I continued watching his hands while this officer was talking to him. You aren't about to catch me slippin'.

Sidenote: you know, one thing I have noticed…actually two things, I have begun to realize about some of these officers: one, while they may be tactically sound, some of them don't have street smarts, and two, common sense ain't common.

The officer, I regretted even responding to the scene to cover, yelled, "Dude, pick up your freakin' tent," as he bent down to grab a corner of the tent. *"Nooooooooo, why? Just let it go,"* I thought. As the officer reached toward the tent, I watched as the guy finally took his hands out of his pocket. While taking his right hand out of his pants pocket, I noticed his face was distorted with anger and frustration.

Before I could say move, I watched as this male violently swung his clenched fist toward the officer, releasing what probably would have been a powerful right upper hook. The way his body twisted when he released the punch made me feel like he was not new to this. As I said earlier, I am a *"Tae Bo"* queen, which means I am basically a black belt at heart; I know what a good punch looks like. Luckily for the officer's sake, the male's first swing was a miss. I almost caught the end of the second swing, which was just as powerful.

Even though he didn't land any of the initial punches, I tried blocking the second punch. What a dummy! We both ended up losing our balance and falling…falling hard on the dirty sidewalk. *"Ouch, why do I always hit my knees first?"* After the impact of the fall, it felt like I was rolling on the ground with this dude. "Put your hands behind your back," I yelled. Now, I am pissed. One, I didn't want to be there in the first place, and two, this could have gone completely different if we just left. There was absolutely no need to escalate this situation.

Still tumbling, I desperately prayed to be out of this situation. My limbs were sprawled out as if I had just got the wind knocked out of me. In the midst of the fight, I started to smell a strong, distinct odor of urine. It was potent, intermingled with the smell of feces. I began sweating profusely for two reasons: this was my fresh, "Monday" uniform, and two, the smell was making me nauseous.

As the male continued to violently flail his arms toward me, trying to punch me with his closed fists, I managed to dodge all hits but one, *"Ouuuccchhhh"* I think he got my nose. I felt this sudden jolt of pain, which caused my eyes to water. For a brief moment, I became dizzy and, I guess you can say, disoriented.

Have you ever been punched in the nose? It's honestly one of the worst places someone can hit you on your face. I mean, this was only the second time I had been punched in the nose, but it's more of the shock factor caused by the impact of the punch. A tear is normally released after that punch. Anyway, now I'm furious. I began administering knee strikes in his torso while giving him commands to *"Stop fighting."*

Eventually, the fighting came to a halt, as he continued lying on his stomach. Although my partner and I had to pry his hands from underneath his body to place him in handcuffs, he appeared to be tired. I mean, I would be too. We successfully placed him in handcuffs. Absolutely no thanks to the officer who started this entire fiasco. Oh, guess what he was doing, standing and watching us fight with this male. Instead of assisting, he watched. I was sooooo done with this dude. Fool me once, shame on you…but you're not fooling me twice. Nope!

We stood up and walked him to our patrol vehicle. During a search incident to arrest, we found a knife in his pocket, which goes back to the main reason I wanted his hands to be visible. If he was detained, I would've just placed him in handcuffs, but at the beginning of the contact, he was not under arrest, and it was not a detention.

As we began driving to jail, the odor of urine and feces filled the car. While explicitly expressing disgust, my partner asked, *"What is that smell?"* ***"Wait, did I step in dog poop,"*** I panicked. I began checking the bottom of my shoes…pheewwww my shoes are clean. I rolled down my window, attempting to remove the disgusting smell that seemed to cling to our patrol vehicle. Yuck, it stinks.

Still surrounded by the pungent odor of feces, I looked at my right bare arm and saw a skid of a brown-colored substance. *No, no noooooooo,* I loudly announced. My stomach started to feel unsettled, like something was swirling inside of it.

I am going to vomit, I thought. My head began to pound, and I began to sweat. *"No, this couldn't be…."* I thought. *"Was I rolling around in…?* No, no, I couldn't have been." My throat began to tighten, and my mouth began to water excessively; it was the increase in saliva when you are about to vomit.

I tried hard to suppress my urge to vomit, only to avoid any additional humiliation. Haven't I been humiliated enough? If you were wondering, I was indeed rolling around in human feces because of Officer Eager Beaver. I had human feces on my upper arm. I can't even believe I am telling you all this. Probably one of the most embarrassing stories I have while being an officer.

Anyway, this was the last time I ever wore a short-sleeved uniform. For the remainder of my career, I wore long-sleeved uniform shirts. I was traumatized.

Tip: Sometimes all you can do is laugh at yourself...oh and maybe check the ground for poop, if you feel there is a possibility the fight will lead to the ground.
This is hard to predict.

Lanah Wright

"10-8"

"No justice, no peace…Know justice, know peace." The protestors chanted as they raised their hand-decorated signs, most of which read, *"Black Lives Matter"* or *"Justice for George Floyd."* The protestors took over the streets, the interstates, and all of downtown, blocking all directions of traffic. Hundreds or maybe thousands of people of all races, backgrounds, and genders, came together to demand change and request solutions. Enough is enough, they chanted!

Some vandalized patrol vehicles. Some of the "looters" took to the streets to begin smashing windows, setting local businesses on fire, and stealing. Our county officials declared a state of emergency. They even imposed overnight curfews across the county.

One night, while working patrol, my partner and I watched as groups of people broke into a local 7-Eleven that had been previously boarded up. Large groups were running out with cases of beer while my squad and I were fighting to put out fires that were set in what felt like every trash can downtown.

We were outnumbered. Plus, I refused to chase someone who stole a case of beer. It ain't worth it.

My squad was at the front of the line for most protests; this one wasn't any different, well, except for the fact that it was declared a civil unrest. So, I guess, in that sense, it was extremely different. In the spring of 2020, we were sent to work a protest in front of our police department headquarters.

Of course, we had additional officers who assisted. Everyone had a task. Everyone was called in to work. No days off for the foreseeable future. "What? Seriously? For the foreseeable future, can they do that?" I asked my co-workers.

Yes, yes, they can, and they did.

As I was saying, my squad, which was comprised of 15 officers, was at the front of the line. All geared up. We stood there with our game faces on. I was the only black person on my team. While I was proud of the community coming together, stepping up, and demanding change, I wanted it to be done correctly. Keeping it peaceful. What I did not agree with were the violent acts toward officers, the looting, the stealing, the vandalism. That was unnecessary, in my opinion.

Anyway, there I was standing in full police riot gear, which meant I had my riot helmet on and was equipped with tools to effectively diffuse all rapidly evolving situations. My squad was trained to ensure demonstrations and protests remained peaceful and lawful assemblies. We also brought such a strong police presence. We made it known that no one was getting through our line to storm our headquarters. Haha! Ew sounds so corny, I know! Even felt awkward writing this, but I am trying to paint the picture for you all.

We were face-to-face with the protestors. *"Traitor…Traitor,"* a group of mixed-race males shouted. *"Like, you aren't even black. How dare you call me a traitor?"* I mumbled under my breath behind my riot helmet.

Amidst the yelling, name-calling, and demands for change, I felt a slight sense of calmness. I was secretly proud of my community. Then, all of a sudden, out of nowhere, *A*

sharp, thunderous "Thump…" followed by "Black Lives Matter…Black Lives Matter" seemed to fill the large, open space.

I watched as heads ducked, the chanting got louder, and then a second thunderous sound of broken glass. *"Ouch!"* A glass bottle hit my boot. *"Who threw that,"* I thought. In reality, I didn't have time to think or question who threw the bottle. Get it together! I looked up and began dodging the food, half-empty water bottles, and rocks being thrown at us.

This was no longer a peaceful assembly.

Nope.

The crowd started advancing toward us. *"Ugh! Great,"* I sighed. *Is this happening?* Loud police announcements ordering people to disperse, in full effect. The crowd chanted louder and louder. Tear gas deployed. I thought, *"Is this what the Rodney King, Los Angeles riots were like?"* Still, no time to truly think.

My adrenaline was on a record high. I experienced this weird adrenaline rush. I wasn't anxious, though; it was this weird feeling of excitement. I was amped up. My heart was racing, and I knew I was mentally prepared to take on this situation. I kind of felt invincible. *"Is this how people feel when they are high?"* Well, the crowd began to disperse after the tear gas was deployed.

Almost 100 arrests that weekend.

What an experience! What a month!

Sigh I never did find that person who threw the bottle at me. At least it hit my boot.

Tip: With all the crap we deal with as law enforcement officers, it is important you create healthy boundaries.
Please try not to take your work home.
Don't be afraid to take self-care days.
The community will thank you!

"10-8"

"F$k the police!"* - 20-year-old black male

I was 10-8[16], minding my own business. *"F*$k the police,"* he yelled while he was standing on the corner, twirling a yellow and green sign that read, *"Street Tacos $2.00."* Instead of yelling anything while I was standing directly in front of him, he yelled this as I rode away on my department-issued, marked police bicycle.

Pause. I know what you are thinking…she's riding a bicycle. Yes, I am, but that's not the point. The point I am addressing is the blatant disrespect for the police. The fact that while he was standing next to his friends, he felt so emboldened to curse the police out.

My partner and I made a quick U-turn on our marked police bicycles and began pedaling in his direction. I started to tightly squeeze my handbrakes as I got closer to the male who felt the urge to speak while we were riding away. The squeezing of my handbrakes caused my rear wheel to skid as I spun my bicycle in front of the male, coming to a skid stop. Okay, you have to see that stop in person. It was actually kind of cool.

Not lame at all.

Once I was standing right in front of the male, I asked, "Wait, sorry…what was that?" The male laughed and looked to his left as if he was waiting for one of his friends to answer, comment, or intervene. My partner followed my

---

[16] Police Code: In service or Available to respond to calls.

question with, "Well, it's clear you wanted our attention, so now you got it."

Shortly after this little interaction, we rode away. For the record, the male was not detained. He was free to leave. We did not request any identification, nor did we instruct him to pull out his Driver's License so we could run his name for warrants. It was simply a conversation…a consensual contact. As a matter of fact, he left the corner with his right arm raised, as he extended his middle finger to flip me off.

Tip: Don't take it personally they can say whatever they want. Brush it off, and if there is the chance for a professional, quick comeback, I'd take it.

"10-8"

_"This is why black people don't like the police." _ – a white
female who was cited for drinking in public.

"This is why black people don't like the police," she
yelled as she walked away after being cited for drinking in
public and having an open container of alcohol.

I know what some of you may be asking: why are you
[police officers] wasting your time issuing citations for open
containers of alcohol instead of solving real crime? Or
maybe this was not the first thought that came to your mind,
but I have honestly lost count of how many times I have
heard that statement.

Nonetheless, I politely asked her to pour out her open
container of alcohol. This was before the citation. My first
intent wasn't to give her a citation.

It was not until, instead of pouring the alcohol out, she
proceeded to drink it in front of my partner and me. The
blatant disrespect. Just pour out the alcohol and be on your
way. I mean, I am all for a good time. I love a good Sunday
brunch with bottomless mimosas, but we aren't in Vegas, and
this is not Sunday brunch.

To be honest with you all, after doing this job for a
while now, I realized a good amount of crime stems from
people being under the influence of drugs or alcohol. It's not
like _"Sunday Funday"_ type drinking…it's more like the
extreme public intoxication level where you are unable to
care for yourself, type drinking. That, right there, folks, is
the drinking that leads to mistakes. She was getting to that
intoxication level, that type of drinking.

Back to the statement made, she yelled, *__This is why black people don't like the police,__* as she walked away with her citation in her hand. I wanted to say, *"Girl, SHUT UP!"* Instead, I looked at her and asked, "Wait, how do you know?" When she turned around to look at me, I noticed she had a smug look on her face, complete with this dumb smirk of amusement. She silently turned back around and walked away.

Alright, I understand there are mixed feelings about law enforcement. I truly do. I recognize there is some truth to this statement. Shoot…half the time, I don't like the police. Hypocrite? Yes, I know! However, in plain clothes, I am treated just like any other black person when viewed through the lens of a chauvinistic white officer, most of the time a white male officer. I don't look like a police officer. In my opinion, I don't think the dislike comes from the lack of appreciation of the role a police officer has in maintaining safety; no, it is deeper than that.

My frustration with this comment stemmed from a white female making comments about a pain she could never possibly truly understand. The statement did not appear to be a genuine concern. There was no empathy or allyship. It was simply a comment made to incite a response and trigger a reaction.

I mean, I still kind of wonder what her response would have been if she had given me the time of day to respond to a legitimate question I had. Like, *"How do you know?"*

On the other hand, I was also being sarcastic. This is honestly my state of being the majority of the time. It's the general tone of most of my responses. I'm not sure if that is a good or bad thing. I am still trying to figure it out.

***Tip:** Don't let comments like these trigger a reaction. That's what they want. Find your inner polite, sarcastic state of being. It helps.*

"10-8"

While I was driving in my patrol vehicle, I heard a female yell, *"You work for the man!"* She yelled this as I came to a stop at a red signal light.

I looked to my right and saw her standing at the side entrance doorway of a homeless shelter. She had her nerve. The fact that she opened her mouth and raised her voice loud enough so I could hear her speak about my employer was crazy. Come talk to me when you have a job. Ah! No! That's messed up, and I don't know her situation.

My next thought was, well damn, at least I work for someone. Okay, also not cool. So, instead, I said nothing; I smiled and waved as I continued driving. Keeping the peace.

This was not the first time I've heard this and I'm sure it won't be the last. I don't work for the man…or maybe I do? I have honestly never truly understood why people say this, especially black people; I mean, we all work for someone, right?

Well, if they [all people making these statements] are referring to the local government, federal government, state, or some sort of authority, then I guess I do work for the man.

Don't we all work for "the man"?

Maybe they are saying that because positions within the local police department are believed to be ostensibly oppressive. Aren't we all somewhat oppressed or controlled by people in positions of power?

I think everyone's experience with *"the man"* will vary based on their circumstances.

Sadly, I think I will be forever confused by this statement, and I am okay with that.

Tip: *Some would say stop working for the man. I'd say, is "the man" paying you? Don't let the man keep you from putting a roof over your head and food on the table. Do you!*

"human"

"No, she doesn't deserve a jacket" - White 50-year-old detective who I don't necessarily care for but will continue to be cordial with.

It was a dark, gloomy, cold winter night. Haha! No, really, though, it was pretty cold and extremely windy. Each gust of wind caused my body to shiver. It was the type of shiver that caused your body to tremble a bit. That uncontrollable shiver. I was wearing a long-sleeved shirt with an outer police vest and tactical pants. Even with all of this equipment on, I was still cold.

"Police with a search warrant, demanding entry," my co-worker loudly announced as we executed a search warrant for a residence where occupants were using, storing, and distributing narcotics, specifically cocaine, in the presence of three children.

Although this case has been adjudicated and all those who should've been convicted were, I won't provide too many details, but I can say it is always extremely heartbreaking to see children brought up in these environments. This is another reason I do what I do: for the babies, those who do not have a choice of what environment they are surrounded by or born into.

Back to the search warrant: after the warrant was executed, the search was complete and all narcotics were seized, the subjects were arrested and placed in the back of separate patrol vehicles.

Before sitting inside the patrol vehicle, one of the subjects asked if we could grab her a jacket before taking her to jail. A reasonable request, I thought. From behind me, my white female co-worker abruptly injected herself into a conversation she was not invited to and disapprovingly said, ***"No, she doesn't deserve a jacket."***

"She doesn't deserve a jacket? It's cold," I replied.

She quickly replied, "Well, we don't know what she has inside of the pockets of the jacket, plus we are about to lock up the house."

Yes, we have found drugs in the pockets of our suspect's clothing during a search incident to arrest, but nothing a thorough search won't fix.

However, this was my case. If I want to get the girl a jacket, I will get her a jacket, *"Cruella,"* I thought. I wish I could've called her Cruella to her face. She is so annoying and just rude!

No, instead, I smiled and slowly said, "We can empty the pockets before handing her a jacket, but I will be grabbing her a jacket." You know, sometimes, when you say things slower, it helps someone better understand the words coming out of your mouth.

C'mon, have some human decency, **Cruella!** Or is that a personal quality that is taught in your childhood and can no longer be obtained once you reach a certain age because you have been a discourteous, inconsiderate, megalomaniac your entire life?

Needless to say, I gave the girl a jacket after thoroughly checking all her pockets.

Tip: *Don't be a discourteous, inconsiderate, megalomaniac. Yes, you are in a position of power, but don't let that go to your head. You are human! It is not a good look.*

"hum n"

"Thank you for being my friend, Officer Wright," a local 40-year-old white homeless man who has been sober for ten years (Former drug of choice, methamphetamine)

I am going to call him "Chris." This was my boy, for real. Christopher was a local homeless man who resided in the city where I worked. The nicest man, with the warmest smile.

While patrolling the downtown area of my city, I would see Chris on street corners or sidewalks, always carrying a duffle bag with him. Chris always wore a beanie, with an oversized t-shirt and jeans. Although he was homeless, I never once saw the expression of defeat on his face. Chris seemed to always have a smile on his face despite the daily trials he presumably encountered as a homeless man in a big city.

Curiosity and empathy urged me to introduce myself to Chris on one of our slower nights downtown. I started by asking how he was doing, to which he replied, "I am blessed." Startled by the response, I smiled.

Chris' response served as a reminder to appreciate the things I normally took for granted. *"Blessed is crazy,"* I thought. It prompted a feeling of guilt. Ima be completely honest with you all; after my first conversation with Chris, I began to question whether I was truly appreciating the blessings and privileges I had.

I kind of felt like I took them for granted. I began to self-reflect. I have a roof over my head, food on my table and I am stressed over things that truly do not matter. *"What truly constitutes a blessed life?"* I thought.

That night was the beginning of our friendship. I'll admit, I truly believe as law enforcement officers we tend to get stuck on that typical police-civilian barrier. We aren't robots. We are human, like everyone else in this city or the city you took an oath to protect and serve. Chris was not just a homeless man; he was human…a man who was homeless.

I made it a point to stop and talk to Chris whenever I had some downtime. I learned Chris became homeless after struggling with his addiction to Methamphetamine. Chris had now been sober for ten years. However, as a result of his addiction, Chris lost his house and his relationship with his parents, wife, and kids. With all this loss, I could not understand how Chris always had a smile on his face.

He was resilient.

I bought Chris coffee on a weekly basis. He didn't eat much but would accept a Subway sandwich from time to time. This was not because I felt bad for Chris; I guess you could say I treated Chris how I would hope to be treated if I were ever in his predicament. It could be any of us.

One night while working downtown, Chris walked up to my partner and me, smiled and said, ***"Thank you for being my friend, Officer Wright."***

A sense of gratitude surrounded me. My heart! Our unlikely friendship was a powerful reminder of the importance of treating others with compassion and generosity. It was a reminder to constantly evaluate my own perspective and priorities, fostering a sense of humility and a greater appreciation for my continued blessings in life.

Thank you for being my friend, Chris.

Tip: *It starts with YOU! Be the change!*

"hum n"

"Give us the f*cking bat" -Hispanic male officer.

There was a homeless male with a bat. I guess what I gathered from the statements taken from all of the witnesses, this male picked up a bat that was tucked in the bushes.

This incident occurred while I was working downtown. The downtown area was a vibrant center of activity. There were three one-way streets that made up our downtown entertainment district. The streets were filled with bars, clubs, restaurants, and hotels. Street vendors lined the corners offering nice, greasy food, flowers, and even cigars. It was a hub for locals and tourists. Friday and Saturday nights brought in a constant flow of people, so I'm sure you could understand why we had over ten calls about this male with a bat.

This male, according to witnesses picked up a bat that was situated in the bushes. Of course, we [police] weren't present when this occurred. The police were called for the report of a male who was causing a disturbance by swinging a bat on the sidewalk as people were passing by. No one was hit, but as you can see, it was a bit concerning.

Upon arrival, I saw a male who matched the description provided by the reporting parties. This male was, in fact, standing on the sidewalk swinging a metal bat. He wasn't just nonchalantly swinging it, though; he was swinging this metal baseball bat with all his might. As the bat was swung through the air, it created that satisfying whooshing sound.

Locals and tourists began walking in the middle of the street to avoid being hit by this bat. I would've done the same thing. As we walked toward the male with the bat, I heard an officer yell, *"Drop the bat."* I watched as the male stopped, lowered the bat toward his right side, but continued to grip the handle of the bat with his right hand.

"Give us the f*cking bat," yelled my Hispanic co-worker. Okay, remember the three-part rule we talked about, you know.

1) Ask... 2) Tell ... 3) Make

Well, we were definitely getting close to the third portion of the rule. I could feel it. We completely skipped the first rule, jumping right to the second one. I noticed my co-worker was visibly frustrated dealing with this guy, and technically, it is not a crime to have a bat, right? With all the phones on us, the concern for the safety of passersby, and the number of calls regarding this male, we had to do something.

I asked the guy if he was hungry. Finally, after repeating my question, he made eye contact with us and replied, "Yeah." I asked if we could make a trade. For this trade, I offered to buy him a bag of chips and soda in exchange for the bat.

There was no immediate response, so I was not even sure if this tactic worked. I watched as he thought about my offer. He replied, "Only if you buy me two cokes and some Cheetos."

Ahhhhh, I gasped, "Deal." He looked at the Hispanic officer as he handed my partner the bat. Okay, this certainly won't work in all situations, and if he said "no," we would've had to think of another creative way to get the bat OR ask him not to swing the bat around people, explaining to him how dangerous it was and how he could possibly hurt someone. I doubt he would've cared and probably would've went back to swinging the bat when we left. That day, we didn't have to worry about it.

We took the bat and put it in our trunk, later impounding it as found property in our evidence room. I walked to the 7-Eleven and purchased two cokes and Cheetos, as requested. I handed the goods to him. He said, "Thanks," and we left. *Sigh* If only every police contact was like this.

Tip: *We, as law enforcement officers, need to work on finding solutions to situations where the use of force can be avoided. You don't necessarily need to spend your money but be creative. Find common ground. You'd be surprised how much can be achieved when you look at conflict creatively.*

"human"

"Get it off me! Get the rat off me!" – a black 50-year-old male under the influence of a controlled substance.

At approximately 7:00 a.m., my partner and I responded to a call regarding a shirtless black male running in and out of traffic. There were multiple 9-1-1 callers on this incident, which led me to believe there was some type of disturbance in that area.

When we read the description provided by the reporting parties, we immediately knew they were describing a chronic narcotics user, whom I will call *"John."* This guy has been arrested for being under the influence of a controlled substance more than a dozen times. Every officer in my division knows John. He has been taken to sobering centers and detox centers, placed on mental illness holds (5150 hold), and booked into jail. His booking alias is *"John "Rat" His Last Name."* Sad, but kind of funny, you will quickly see why.

Keep reading.

John was unemployed and homeless. Whenever he chose to ingest a controlled substance he created some type of public disturbance because, one, the effects of the drugs always led him to be erratic and paranoid, and two, the drugs were always ingested in a public place.

This day was not any different.

Upon arrival, I saw John standing on the corner, yelling extremely rapid, incoherent statements. He was still shirtless. Mentally, John's behavior was altered. I have seen him sober. He was a pretty cool guy, but has struggled with his addiction to crack cocaine for almost 15 years.

I have had conversations with John about getting clean, but John described his withdrawals as an intense pain with symptoms *"too hard to kick."* He used to be married with kids, but got addicted to crack cocaine and probably other drugs. He once mentioned he was clean for two days but relapsed to get rid of the state of turmoil his mind and body went through as the drug withdrawals transpired.

Can you imagine being unable to resist the grip of a drug addiction that your life begins to unravel, and you begin to spiral into chaos? It's sad. A piece of me felt bad for John. I guess having conversations with him in his sober state of mind has allowed me to see that he is more than his addiction.

But today…today, John was clearly under the influence of a controlled substance.

Every time he smoked crack cocaine, he appeared to be agitated and paranoid. He was never able to sit still or focus and was unable to engage in a simple conversation.

My partner and I exited our patrol vehicle and went to speak with John. Sadly, he had been through this process far too many times. Without hesitation, John placed his hands behind his back and started ducking. He kept his head low and his shoulders hunched as if he was hiding from someone. "Ahhh!" he yelled. His movements were quick, furtive, and unpredictable.

John's forehead was glistening, with droplets of sweat rolling down the front and sides of his face. I imagine his sweat was salty. You know when you are working out and sweat drips down your forehead, and the beads of sweat begin to form on your lips, and you happen to taste it because you are so deep in your workout that you don't have time to wipe your face in that moment. It's always so salty, so I've heard. Well, that's what John was going through. I wondered if he even noticed.

Anyway. When I placed John in handcuffs, his hands were clammy and wet. Yuck! Yuck! Yuck! At least I had gloves on. Since John was shirtless, I noticed all the large beads of sweat dripping down his back.

As I walked John to our patrol vehicle, he yelled, at the top of his lungs, ***"Get it off me! Get the rat off me!"***

"John, there aren't any rats on you," I replied. Looking terrified, he jumped and uttered, "It's right there...Ahhhh," as he looked at his right shoulder.

At this point, I had to play along. Otherwise, this extreme paranoia and episode of hallucinations would continue the entire ride to jail.

I decided to humor John and began dusting off his right shoulder. "There, the rat is gone." John looked at his right shoulder and took a slow, deliberate, deep breath. As he exhaled, his body looked like it had just released pent-up stress.

"It worked," I thought. Although he was still high and rambled the entire ride to jail, at least he no longer had rats on him.

---

*Tip: John struggled with his drug addiction, but let's be real, we all struggle with something. Some are better at hiding it than others. **You are not perfect. Don't act like you are.** We should strive to treat everyone with compassion, well, unless they are a**holes.*

Yikes! She thinks he is hallucinating
CRACK IS WACK!

"human"

> ***"I would never spend my money on them"*** -white male officer.

My partner and I just responded to a check the welfare call regarding a 40-year-old male and his 4-year-old son. As we approached the intersection where they were seen sitting, I noticed a young boy sitting on a blanket that was placed on the sidewalk. The blanket was folded. I believe they folded it to ensure they weren't blocking the sidewalk, preventing passersby from utilizing the sidewalk.

I approached the boy and his father and introduced myself. The father mentioned they were on the waitlist for a homeless shelter, as both he and his wife had lost their jobs, causing them to lose their small apartment. The little boy was not at the age where he should've been in school. His body was not frail, and he did not appear to suffer from malnourishment; he opened a bag of chips while we were speaking with his dad.

While my partner was speaking with the father, I asked the little boy if he was hungry. Without hesitation, he immediately looked at his dad and said, "No." I watched as my partner provided the 40-year-old male with a list of homeless shelters, along with resources for children.

While we were speaking with the father, I noticed a female holding what appeared to be an iPhone. While holding the iPhone, I watched as she extended her right hand out toward us. She proudly raised the phone higher, as if she was trying to intimidate me or maybe secretly said, *"Look at me; I'm recording you. I am big and bad."* As she continued to record, people passing by began to take notice of her recording and started stopping to watch. Some even pulled out their phones to record. *"What are they recording,"* I thought.

"So annoying," I uttered under my breath. We are in a world where pulling out your phone to record any type of incident with police interactions is normal.

Still weird.

I could see if she was attempting to record to obtain evidence of any police misconduct, but that was not the case. Maybe she intended to bring awareness about the issue of homelessness to inspire others to take action to put an end to homelessness. Maybe?

As we cleared the scene, she yelled, "Look, the cops aren't going to do anything. What are we paying you for? The kid is homeless." Well, at this point in the book, I think it is important to clarify that homelessness itself is not a crime. It is indeed a complex issue that affects many, including children, but it is not a crime.

While walking toward our patrol vehicle, I responded, "It is not a crime to be homeless, Ma'am." I got in the car quick enough to avoid subjecting myself to any other response from this very annoying lady. Between you and me, my heart ached for that kid; it truly did. Even though the kid said he wasn't hungry, and the parents were able to feed their son, I felt like I should get him something to eat for dinner to eliminate some of the stressors the parents may have had as they attempted to make ends meet and because every kid deserves a "happy meal."

It was my partner's day to drive, so I asked if he could stop by McDonald's. My partner looked confused. He knew I didn't eat McDonald's; I was on a healthy kick. Once we reached the window to order, I ordered a "Happy Meal" and a "Big Mac" meal, nothing extravagant, but still something. We drove back to the intersection where the kid and his father were seated. I stepped out of the vehicle and handed them the food.

They smiled and thanked me.

When I was giving the family the McDonald's, a fellow officer drove by my partner and me. I made eye contact with this officer and acknowledged him with a *"what's up"* head nod as he drove away. At the end of the shift, he walked to our patrol vehicle, laughed, and said, ***"I would never spend my money on them."***

This dude is one of the most entitled men in the department. He seemed to believe that every single person owed him something because of his self-perceived status of superiority. I simply smiled and replied, "Good thing it was not your money!"

I guess some people, like this co-worker, wonder why I am willing to buy someone a meal here and there. When I thought about why, I believe it is because growing up, I witnessed my parents never hesitate to spare a couple of bucks on food for those less fortunate than us.

Plus, in Isaiah 58:7, the Bible says, *"Is it not to share your food with the hungry and to provide the poor wanderer with shelter; when you see the naked, to clothe him, and to not turn away from your own flesh and blood."*

Even though I own a Keurig, I spend $5.00 on coffee at least four out of the seven days of the week. I am not rich, but I can spare a couple of dollars.

*Tip: As Michael Jackson sang, if you want to make the world a better place, take a look at **yourself** and then make a change. That's all it takes...if we all do it.*

"i am the police"

*"**Yoooooo she got my balls,**"– a 21-year-old male with an outstanding felony warrant for assault with a deadly weapon.*

In the middle of the shopping center, the mall promenade to be exact, a fight unfolded between a 21-year-old male riding a "BMX[17]" style bicycle, myself, and my partner.

Let me back up. It was not an actual street fight, but this guy was actively resisting because he did not want to go to jail. Of course this was an assumption, but just read what happened and judge for yourself.

My partner and I were walking through the promenade on foot. We had been getting complaints about armed robberies of pedestrians at this promenade, which is why our police captain requested extra patrol. We were on it.

While standing in the center of the promenade, we observed a male riding a "BMX-style" bicycle through the promenade. Okay, in the state I am in, this is a violation of the vehicle code section, which bicyclists do, in fact, fall under. The vehicle code prohibits bicycle riding on the sidewalk and through the promenade. Furthermore, there were city signs posted everywhere prohibiting the riding of a bicycle on promenade grounds.

---

[17] A road style bicycle used for stunt riding and tricks. These bikes normally had big handle bars and pegs.

We conducted a pedestrian stop of the black male who was riding his bicycle through the promenade. I identified myself as a police officer, even though I was in full police uniform. You'd be surprised how many times I have heard, *"I didn't know you were a cop,"* even though I am driving a marked patrol vehicle and wearing a uniform that clearly identifies me as a police officer.

I digress.

We conducted a pedestrian stop of the male. At first, he was compliant. He stopped and began straddling the bicycle, with both of his feet planted on the ground. His hands were still grasping the handlebars, with his fingers wrapped around the torn rubber grips.

When I asked for identifying information, he provided his name without any hesitation. Before letting this guy leave with a warning to walk his bicycle through this area of the mall, I conducted a routine records check. The records check revealed there was an outstanding felony warrant for his arrest.

He couldn't hear anything our dispatch said, but I guess, based on our body language, he knew what was up. I calmly requested the male to put his hands behind his back and explained to him that there was an active warrant for his arrest.

Wait, before we get into it, let me tell you what **my first mistake was…I should've had him get off the bicycle before attempting to place him in handcuffs.** What a dummy! Me, I am the dummy.

He refused to place his hands behind his back. Remember the *"ask, tell, make"* rule…well we quickly escalated to the **make** rule when his front tire rolled over my foot as he attempted to ride away. Luckily my partner and I were each on one side of the bicycle.

We each grabbed one of his forearms and attempted to **make** him place his hands behind his back. The male had this sudden burst of violent aggression, and out of nowhere, I could feel my body falling toward the ground…with the male and his bicycle.

To be honest, everything seemed to slow down as I started to brace myself as I was falling. My right knee struck the ground first, breaking my fall. I felt this intense, shocking pain shoot through my limbs once my knees hit the concrete. *"Oh, my gosh, why must I always fall on my knees?"*

My partner and I gave this guy multiple loud commands to place his hands behind his back, but he refused. His arms were flailing in a desperate attempt to release himself from our hold. While on the ground, he started using his legs to kick my partner and me. Due to our close proximity, I was never severely kicked, or if I was, I didn't feel it. It was probably the adrenaline flowing through my veins.

After a brief struggle, he was back on his feet. *What the....?* He started swinging his clenched fist toward my partner. I watched as my partner ducked after the first swing and tried to guide this guy to the ground. I saw my partner wrap his arms around the male's upper body, so I went toward the male's shins. Together, we were able to safely get this guy on the ground, which was a position of disadvantage for him at the moment. All I wanted to do was place this guy in handcuffs.

WHY ARE YOU RESISTING?

Passersby stopped, and a crowd began to form. I didn't notice this crowd at first. **The second mistake I made, always be aware of your surroundings**. At this point, my heart rate was increasing, my breathing was becoming rapid and shallow, and, of course, I was sweating. I hate sweating underneath my vest. Yuck!

This guy wouldn't stop. Every technique we used did not work. If my partner, a male who was approximately 5'11, weighing approximately 195-200 lbs. **(Disclaimer- I am not good at *guesstimating* weight)** with exceptional physical strength and mental toughness could not get this guy to place his hands behind his back then I did not think my physical strength was going to help. I am strong, but I am also realistic.

Within seconds, I did it. I used my hands to grab and squeeze his … sigh…his genitals. I instructed him again to put his hands behind his back, to which he immediately complied while yelling, ***"Yoooooo she got my balls!"***

Finally, we were able to place him in handcuffs and transport him to jail after a stop at the hospital. He had a complaint of pain in his groin area.

I had a complaint of pain to my entire body. I think I had a knot on my forehead from hitting my head on the handlebar of his stupid bicycle.

What felt like 30 minutes of fighting was actually only two minutes. Insane right?

***Tip:** You have to do what you have to do.
Fight smarter, not harder.
Technique always wins.*

"i am the police"

"You can't have official meetings without me" – 50–60-year-old white male sergeant that should retire.

Not gonna lie, there are some people who chose to be police officers because they sought control. They are individuals who thrive on control. The type of overbearing, power-hungry people, I described earlier in this book. My sergeant at the time was one of them. Most people think I left the unit because of him. Not true. However, he did make my life miserable while working for him. Everyone saw it, but no one spoke up. Even my lieutenant attempted to comfort me by saying, *"He will retire soon. Just hang in there."*

I actually liked this lieutenant, but I always wondered why he never stood up to my sergeant after numerous independent complaints, not from me, but from others in the department. Sadly, that was the culture with policing, suck it up and just take it; remain in an environment where you are unhappy…because, well…job security.

I worked in the narcotics unit for a bit. There, I worked on cases involving drug dealers. I worked undercover on several different occasions, buying narcotics from street-level dealers.

In a long-term operation, I would buy drugs from this local grocery store. Word on the street was everyone inside of the grocery store was in on it.

The clerks at the check-out stand washed the money, and the grocery store had lookouts[18] on every corner. Supposedly, they stored the drugs in the back of the store. Community members were scared of the people who hung out in that area and had to drive out of their way to go to other grocery or convenience stores because most of the community was not welcome at this particular grocery store.

To make things worse, there were numerous shootings in that grocery store parking lot, and most of the people who hung out in that area to sell drugs were documented gang members.

While working undercover, I bought a few grams of cocaine from these dudes and I did it often. They never suspected anything because, well, I fit in. I could *"talk the talk"* and *"walk the walk."* I guess that was a good thing. One guy even told me he *"pimps hoes"* he said it as if I should've been excited. Like I should've jumped at the opportunity to take his number. I mean, I did take his number. I went back and conducted a records check of the number he provided so I could identify him. He actually had been arrested for pimping and pandering. Wow, he was being honest.

Most of these men carried firearms. I would see them as they dug in their crouch area to grab the baggy of loose rocks of crack cocaine or the baggie of cocaine to sell to me. At this point, I imagine I probably lost you. Yes, I know people are still selling and using crack cocaine. Crazy? Well, not for them. It was $20.00 for a small rock of crack and even more for a gram of cocaine. I didn't understand the hype, but they were making money.

---

[18] A person or group of people posted at a location with the sole responsibility of observing everything and to report everything seen or heard to avoid detection by law enforcement.

I purchased lots of crack cocaine, cocaine, and methamphetamine in an undercover capacity. I had real-life conversations with the majority of these men. They gave me their nicknames and would remind me they *"banged."* I am not sure if this was an intimidation tactic, but I listened.

After a few months of buying drugs from several different people, we had several street-level dealers to indict. I was a part of a grand jury indictment. Now, I didn't do this alone; there were a few other officers who helped, so we shared the task of going undercover. One of them played as my cousin, so I was able to introduce him to a few of my plugs[19] so that next time, he could go solo and buy drugs without me present. I vouched for him, and they accepted it.

In prepping for the big arrest day, I decided to be proactive and reach out to a detective and sergeant who worked in the gang's unit. Yes, I could've told my micromanaging sergeant, but he repeatedly showed me he could care less about anything else I did. Most of the time he only spoke to my partner, who was a Trump-loving, Colin Kaepernick-hating, black history month disbelieving, 45-year-old white man. *(Despite the differences we had, I actually liked my partner. He had a good heart. We just disagreed on a lot of things…almost everything.)*

Anyway, I could've told my sergeant but I did not. I was a competent detective who could work my own cases and speak to whomever I wanted to. I was not going behind his back or jumping the chain of command. I was simply going to speak with people to get their advice. They [gang unit] have a little more experience investigating and working with gangs, hence why they were assigned to the gang unit.

---

[19] Someone who is a resource for obtaining something valuable that would otherwise be difficult to obtain; like drugs.

As I exited the elevator to walk toward the entrance of the gang unit I turned the corner and who did I see…yup you guessed right, well hopefully you did…it was my sergeant. He was turning the corner walking toward the elevator lobby.

My heart sank. I could feel my heart drop to my stomach. I know I didn't do anything wrong, but just knowing the type of person he was I knew he was going to ask where I was going. As we both got closer to the entrance door of the gang unit he extended his arm across the entrance door, essentially blocking my path of entering.

In this patronizing, condescending voice, he asked, *"Where are you going, missy?"*

"Missy? What am I 12?" I thought. "Um, I am going to talk to Julie," I stuttered. I was not scared, but I just never really had someone physically prevent me from entering an office, an office I was in fact allowed to be in.

He huffed and puffed, kind of like the big, bad scary wolf did before blowing the three little pigs' houses down and sternly responded, ***"You can't have official meetings without me."*** News Flash. Earth to my knucklehead sergeant, I actually can. I am not doing anything wrong. I smirked and replied, "It's not an official meeting."

As I mentally prepared myself to walk under his arm, I saw all this armpit hair protruding from his short-sleeved t-shirt opening. Ew!

I began to lean back slightly as I walked under his arm as if we were playing a game of limbo, and he was using his arm as the stick. However, we weren't playing a game. It wasn't even an enjoyable experience.

Technically, I could've gone to internal affairs to file a complaint against my sergeant for creating a hostile work environment by using intimidation techniques and preventing me from entering an office by physically blocking me.

I didn't. Instead, I shared it with you all. Some will tell you to report the incident. Some will call you a snitch if you do. I can't tell you one way or another, but I will say you need to do what is best for you. Like my aunt used to tell me, "What they think of you is none of your business." I take this quote with me everywhere I go because it is so true.

Let us not forget that some officers and sergeants think they are above the law. Those who thrive on power and control. Not everyone is like them, but they sure are out there. Be careful and tread with caution, but always stand your ground.

***Tip:** Always do what is best for YOU. Whatever that is. People are going to talk, regardless. Half of them will never be put in scenarios you will be or have been put in. It's just the facts.*

"i am the police"

"I hate you negro. You want to be white. That's why you talk like that." – Yells a 40-year-old biracial female

She yelled this as my partner, a white male, and I were leaving our favorite coffee shop. This was at the start of our 12-hour shift. We worked the overnight shift, so before you ask, *"Is this what the taxpayers were paying for?"* let me explain to you…yes, this is what the taxpayers were paying for. We are getting coffee. Give us a break.

Anyway.

This lady was one of the local homeless people in the area. We [patrol officers] have dealt with her on several different occasions. There were times when she barked at me as I walked by…like a loud, aggressive dog-like bark. I am never too sure how to respond to these barks so I don't, I don't respond at all. Just keep walking.

On one occasion, she bit an officer on my squad while he was trying to place her in handcuffs. In a completely separate incident, this lady tried to spit on me. If you have never been spat at let me tell you, it is an extremely unpleasant experience. So disrespectful. If you did not know, it's technically considered assault, as it should be. Gross! The act itself is degrading and demeaning. How low can you go…wait never mind, this lady could go low.

I hate to call people crazy, but, um...she was a bit bizarre and somewhat odd.

I never knew why she didn't like me, but judging all of our encounters, it was clear she was not fond of me.

As a black female officer, I found that I am often the subject of insults. Unlike the majority of my co-workers, I'm not just insulted for being an officer. Most get to choose what type of insult they want to throw at me, being a black officer, a female officer, being black, or just being an officer. This lady chose the black path.

As if spitting on me or biting one of my partners was not enough, she locked eyes with me as my partner and I were leaving our favorite coffee shop. She continued to stare me down, probably attempting to make me feel uncomfortable. As I shared with you all earlier, I don't get uncomfortable during stare contests. I will win. Always.

Well, as she fixed her eyes on me, with her cold, emotionless piercing gaze she yelled, ***"I hate you negro. You want to be white. That's why you talk like that."*** She had this self-satisfied, smug smirk on her face as she insulted me. The type of smirk that revealed her two front teeth, the only two teeth that she had. She took pleasure in verbally attacking me, attempting to make me feel powerless. It was like she had just received a small piece of satisfaction, kind of like she had just won an award.

After her statement, I laughed. I found the insult pretty funny. I love being black. I also tend to respond to situations like these with humor. Okay, for all my psychologists, I am not trying to mask my hurt feelings. There really is no deeply rooted reason why I respond with laughter except the simple fact that I refuse to let insults like these bother me.

I am also used to being told I don't talk "black." Let me ask you something…what is talking black? I mean, is there only one way for someone to speak based on their color? Why do we do this? It is not just on the white community, it's on the black community as well.

Anyway. I laughed and walked away. As I entered my patrol vehicle, I smiled at her and said, "Have a great day." In a contemptuous manner, she retorted, "Whatever," as she left in the opposite direction.

If she was a nice person, I probably would've considered buying her coffee, but there are some times when I just can't go high, this was one of those times. Sorry, Mrs. Michelle Obama.

Tip: *This job is already difficult. We see and experience things that most people will never experience, which is why you should ALWAYS allow yourself the space to laugh because a day without laughter is a day wasted. For real!*

"i am the police"

> *"...My moral values will not allow me to justify the killing of our people (historically and currently) in the name of our friendship." –My <u>former</u> friend of 10 years*

On Wednesday, I sent one of my former ~~friends~~ (herein referred to as '**FF**') a link, which was sent to me by my sister.

<u>Can Black Lives Matter & Law Enforcement See Eye to Eye?"-Middle Ground (YouTube)</u>

The creator of this episode brought together law enforcement and Black Lives Matter supporters together to spark a conversation surrounding not only the differences, but similarities both groups had.

Although I think you should watch this YouTube clip, if watching interferes with reading this book, then I'd choose the latter. So, instead, I will sum up the YouTube clip for ya.

It went a little something like this: the narrator would present a thought-provoking, possibly contentious statement or question about race and law enforcement. I'll give you an example of the statement presented during this clip, *"I regularly fear for my life."* The participants then get to choose whether or not they *regularly fear for their lives* by picking one side over the other.

Once each participant chose their side, they had the opportunity to share why they chose one side over the other. It's kind of like that team-building activity called *"Cross the line,"* I think most of us have either participated in this activity at school or in the workplace.

Why did I send this link? Well, I sent this because I believed it was a thought-stimulating clip. It was not sent in hopes that watching this would change her perspective of policing in America. It was not sent with the belief that one video could suddenly erase the issues of systemic racism and inequality that are so deeply rooted in our country. It was sent from one friend to another friend. I sent it because I thought it was a thought-provoking video and I wanted to share it with a friend. Is that wrong?

Boy oh boy was I wrong! Before I get into the aftermath of sending this text, I want to share with you our relationship prior to this. I was presented with a few red flags, but nothing earth-shattering, or so I thought.

We met in college and were inseparable. We built a bond that I believed would withstand anything life threw our way.

After undergraduate and graduate school, we took different paths in life, and I chose the Criminal Justice field. At first I thought, despite our chosen paths we still respected one another. Every now and then, she would slip a shady comment or subtle jab into our conversation.

<u>Example / Red flag #1[20]:</u>

Me: This guy tried to fight my partner and me today.

FF: What did you do?

Me: Huh? Nothing, he had a warrant and didn't want to go to jail.

FF: *Silence*

This is when it started. I slowly started to feel the once unwavering support of my FF starting to waver. *Why am I being blamed? Are you going to ask me if I was alright?* I thought. This conversation lasted approximately 45 minutes, but ended with a mutual understanding to which we agreed to disagree.

Time passed. I felt myself walking on eggshells when talking about my career. Constantly trying to avoid anything work-related, good or bad. I started feeling uneasy around her, but I still wanted to support her. I mean, she was not a bad person. We just didn't see eye to eye.

The following year was her graduate school celebration. Myself and a few of her other friends flew down to support and celebrate her. I was excited simply because, one, we were celebrating a huge accomplishment and two, I was able to meet her new graduate school friends.

Before I introduced myself, my FF pulled me to the side and attempted to prep me essentially saying, <u>Red flag #2:</u> *"Hey, can you not tell them you're a cop? They don't*

---

[20] The term red flag is a metaphor. It is generally used as a warning or a cause for concern that there is a problem with a certain situation like this friendship.

really f%&k with law enforcement. I don't want this to become a huge discussion." I rolled my eyes, took a deep breath and responded, *"Okay."*

It's her day, right? I continued to remind myself that I was there for her while I experienced a surge of adrenaline.

I didn't speak that entire night. I just sat there listening to everyone talk, while looking up flights to head home early. However, with the advice of my sister, I did end up staying for the graduation, but the vibe was indeed off.

So that was a little background of our friendship as of recent. Back to the YouTube link: **Can Black Lives Matter & Law Enforcement See Eye to Eye?"-Middle Ground (YouTube)**. Shortly after sending this YouTube link, she asked, "Why would you send that to me?" Of course, I became defensive, "What is wrong with me sending it to you?" She essentially replied, *honestly, I don't care about what they have to say, and I am not going to waste my time watching some YouTube clip with uneducated people talking about stuff they know nothing about. The criminal justice system is flawed and was not built for our people, and you chose that career.*

As emotions seemed to run high, our conversation turned into an argument. My voice grew louder as I responded, "Wow, the education system was not built for us and you chose that career. What career was built for us to succeed? Huh?" Our phone conversation ended after she shared a story about an off-duty, black officer who was beaten up by white male officers when he tried to assist them with taking a male into custody.

After we hung up the phone, she sent me the article. I read it. Here are a few points she left out:

1) The off-duty black male officer did not identify himself when he intervened. As an officer, black or white, if you see other officers fighting to try to take someone into custody, you should identify yourself by presenting your badge. This is in no way saying the white officers were in the right, but why would you ever jump into a fight without letting them know you're an officer? That's just dumb;

2) The black officer was off duty, in plain clothes, again with nothing that visibly identified himself as someone with the police. He jumped in to assist officers in full police uniform without any police identification. This goes back to point one, and lastly;

3) The off-duty black officer was armed. He could've been shot! Black or not, if you jump in to assist my partner and me with placing someone in handcuffs without identifying yourself, and I have never seen you before, which is common when you work for a large agency, and you have a firearm, my first thought is you're trying to harm me or my partner. Period.

Clearly, she did not do her research before sending this article. That's okay, though. I dissected the article with my sister, I had to make sure I wasn't tripping.

Once I collected my thoughts, I provided every detail she missed in the article. Like, girl, did you read it? I did not say that directly, but my response said everything.

She essentially replied, <u>Red flag #3:</u> *The interpersonal level is what allowed me to see you as Lanah; the structural forces remind me, regardless, you are part of a system that historically kills our people, and I will never be a part of that."*

We didn't speak for days. Days turned into weeks, and silence began to fill the void between us. Our friendship was fading away, and I wanted to believe I was kind of okay with it. I mean, I did miss our trips, the laughter, our conversations and the companionship we once had, but I felt we needed our space.

Then bam…the murder of George Floyd.

I suppose it is somewhat tough for some to grasp that emotions from being affected by the murder of George Floyd and being a police officer during that time can coexist. Yes, I was a police officer, but I was also black, which is why I found myself in a state of internal turmoil.

I was grappling with a mix of emotions following the murder and found myself relying more and more on my support group. I struggled to put on my police uniform, almost in tears when I had to go to work. I started to get that knot in my stomach and felt nauseous whenever I pulled up to the parking lot gate. My racing thoughts never seemed to quiet down, and these days, they were louder than normal, constantly bombarding my mind with negative thoughts and scenarios, so this was the last thing I needed.

While getting ready for work, I received text messages from my FF. The text messages essentially read:

Witnessing the murder of George Floyd today by the hands of you and your people has deeply affected me emotionally and created a space that I can't really think

My moral values will not allow me to justify the killing of our people (historically and currently) in the name of our friendship.

I did not respond. I blocked her and never looked back.

As my dad, a wise black man shared with me after I cried to my parents about this incident, *"Baby, you don't want people that don't support you in your life. Forget her."*

So, FORGET THEM! Whomever they are. You need to protect your peace. If this or any position you are in is what God has called you to do and you truly believe you are living in your purpose, then you be the best law enforcement officer or [insert your job title here] you can be!

Not gon' lie, this situation was tough. Just remember, if you stay in environments where people don't recognize the value of YOU, you will almost always shrink. I learned the hard way, but I learned. I am not mad or upset at my FF. I just know she was unable to show up the way I wanted and needed her to show up and that's okay.

No hard feelings.

Tip: Some people in our lives have an expiration date. Sometimes, the blessing is just that.

"i am the police"

"All cops are bastards, especially the cop you're related to!" - 19-year-old black female / former friend of 4 years.

Yikes. While aimlessly scrolling through Instagram when I still had one, I came across one of my sorority sister's Instagram stories. The story had a black background with bold red writing inscribed across the post. It read, *"All cops are bastards, especially the cop you're related to"* Wow! It even had the animated Mickey Mouse hand with a finger pointing at me or whoever opened her story to view her post.

Okay? Well, I blocked her. It started this block rampage I took on. I started blocking *"all lives matter"* people, the *"non-law enforcement friendly"* people, and even the *"look/view but don't like or comment"* people. It got easier and easier by the block.

That was it. I didn't offer a long-drawn-out excuse as to why I was blocking them. It wasn't needed and it felt so good. So satisfying.

Yes. I chose me. I advise you to do the same.

Tip: B-L-O-C-K THEM!! BLOCK THEM!!
Protect your peace.

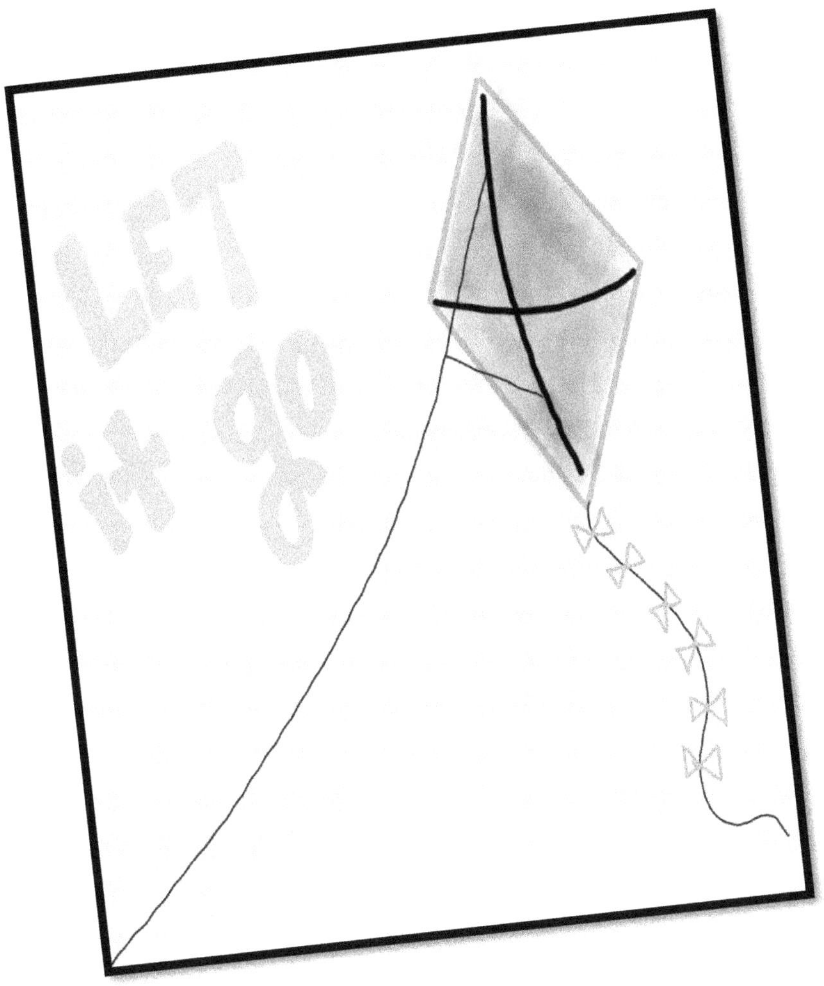
LET
it go

"i am the police"

"Wait, do you remember me?" - 21-year-old employee.

"Welcome" the male behind the counter yelled at the top of his lungs as we entered our favorite local coffee shop. Taken aback, I softly replied, "Hi…uh, thanks." I doubt he even heard me, but I always feel rude if I do not reply. Do you find it weird when employees yell "welcome" as you enter the door to their place of employment? I mean, can I at least get inside the store? It's a bit obnoxious if you ask me. At least wait until I am closer so I don't have to yell back. I don't know, that's just my opinion.

Anyway….at the beginning of each shift, my partner and I would stop by our favorite local coffee shop to grab a "pick me up" drink before work. We would begin our shift with a quad espresso. The local coffee shop called it the "Quad." This coffee shop had become a cherished place for not only the community but also our police department.

As we approached the counter, the scent of freshly brewed coffee immediately comforted me. I began to place my order but could not help but notice the female behind the counter staring at me. When I looked toward her, I noticed her eyes began to widen as she tilted her head. "Do I know her?" I felt a sense of confusion as I tried to figure out if I knew this girl or if she was confused. After placing our orders, we walked toward the pick-up counter to wait for our coffee. While my partner and I were talking, I noticed the female begin to walk toward me…without our coffee. I braced myself for the possibility of a tense interaction. She was not walking toward me with a smile, so I was unsure how this conversation was going to go.

"Good morning! Long time no see," she uttered. I am sure I had a blank stare on my face as I replied, "Hi" while I tried to place where I knew her from. Still nothing. I mean, she kind of looked familiar…or was it my brain distorting my thoughts, leading me into believing I did recognize her? Feeling awkward for not remembering her, I tried to engage in the conversation as best as I could. With the expression of disappointment across her face, she asked, ***"Wait, do you remember me?"***

Ugh, my heart sank knowing I had to be honest in my response. I had no idea who she was and am pretty good with remembering faces…um, "Sorry, I don't." She smiled and replied, "You, your partner, and a CPS worker came to my apartment. I had a restraining order against my baby's father, who I let hide in the bedroom closet because he had a felony warrant." She whispered, "I let my baby's father back into my apartment, even though there were several incidents of him hitting me while I was holding my baby. The CPS worker took my baby from me that day."

When she began sharing her story, I immediately remembered her. This was the first time I witnessed CPS take a child from their mother, even I was low-key traumatized by just witnessing the incident. I watched this mother scream and cry as she watched helplessly as her baby was placed inside the CPS vehicle and taken away. I could not imagine the reality and pain of losing a child to CPS, but I was informed it would only be temporary as long as the mother demonstrated her commitment to her child's safety. It was sad, and, at that moment, I forgot that she had lied to us, yelled at us, and cursed at us, all while allowing her boyfriend to hide from us in her bedroom closet. That day, I even tried to comfort her as she cried… shoot I even hugged this girl!

After she was done speaking, I hesitantly asked, "How is your baby?" I instantly regretted asking this question…I mean, what if she never got her baby back? I awkwardly waited for her response. She smiled and replied, "I got a job at this coffee shop, completed my counseling and parenting classes, and now have full custody of my baby. We are doing great."

Aw, that is so good to hear. I am glad. I was rooting for you!

"Lanah, your Quad," the loud, obnoxious man behind the counter yelled. As the conversation began to come to an end, she quickly said, "Thank you for that day." I smiled and replied, "No problem."

Tip: Always be compassionate. Life is hard, we never really know what battle the next person may be fighting.

"triple threat"

If you read the entire book…instead of skipping to the end *(I'm joking),* you are probably thinking dang, she went through a lot of crap. Make no mistake, on some days I did, but because of my supportive family and friends I learned how to not let the various challenges define me. My story is unfortunately way too common in law enforcement. I have only highlighted a few of the numerous challenges officers face, both personally and professionally. These challenges can take a toll on your mental and emotional well-being, for real. Don't take that lightly!

One of my favorite sergeants once pulled me to the side and said, "While ninety percent of people appreciate and respect the work (police officers) do, there is that ten percent that do not and will not like you because you're wearing that uniform." He was right.

As a matter of fact, we aren't really dealing with that ninety percent of the community. They aren't the ones causing the issues. These are the ones that will *"thank you for your service"* as they walk past you. The same ones who will try their hardest to get your attention…not to report a crime, but to extend their hand toward you to shake yours. This is why I do it, for that ninety percent.

This is what makes it such a rewarding career. Knowing that you're making a difference, regardless of how small it seems in your eyes. Regardless of how much crap you take. Therefore, in those times when you feel like giving up, **always, always, always** remember why you chose your career. Change starts from within. Lead by example, and continue to treat everyone with respect, even those who don't deserve it.

Throughout my law enforcement career, I've met some incredible police officers, some amazing people, both in the community and in the department, and a few individuals I will remain friends with for life. On the contrary, I have also met some…not so amazing people; those people provided me with some of the content I have shared with you all throughout this book.

I hope my collection of experiences shared through these short stories helped readers understand the emotions of some officers, emotions that are often misunderstood, especially when it comes to people of color and more specifically, black women.

Most importantly, I hope I was able to give a voice to many unspoken experiences of not only black female officers but officers of color, both men and women and female officers everywhere.

And so, you, my amazing, empathetic, beautiful/handsome readers, I will leave you with some of my last tips, **Tips** that kept and continue to keep me motivated.

- We fight our toughest battles on our knees PRAY ABOUT IT;
- When in conflict, be sarcastic with your remarks. Always laugh when you can, life is too short to take things personally;
- You need your allies and support system. You can start the change, but you can't do it alone;
- It's okay to feel. In this profession, we seem to be conditioned to think you aren't a good officer because you show emotions. Nah, let's break this cycle. You are not a robot;
- Always choose your mental health;
- This world is temporary. Leave it better than you found it;
- Be gentle with yourself. Continue to water YOU; and lastly
- Be intentional with your moves, your thoughts, and your words.

YOU ARE A TRIPLE THREAT!

Wherever you are, whatever field you are in, I truly believe you are here for a reason

To my Black and Brown, Female or Male, Police Officers or <u>Insert YOUR Job Title/Career Here</u>

You have immense and innate value in this world

We (Black & Brown women and men) are powerful beyond measure

DON'T LET EM' TELL YOU OTHERWISE.

Stay blessed y'all 

"acknowledgments"

This book started as a string of ideas that would have been lost in translation if it weren't for the love, support, and encouragement of my tribe.

Thank you:

Most importantly, my amazing parents; your unwavering belief in me has always been my constant source of inspiration. Daddy, my heavenly angel, this book is for you. I finally finished. I hope I made you proud.

Mommy, for helping me share my experiences with the world. For not only reading and editing the first completed draft, but listening to me read chapters aloud, and providing honest feedback, even when I did not ask for it (j/k). Your encouragement not only during my writing process but throughout my life is indispensable.

My amazing sisters-my first best friends: seeing you ladies navigate through life inspires me to keep going. Thank you for always being my safe space, a space filled with laughter and comfort, one where I can retreat when things get rough and life gets…well, difficult. I love you and can't imagine life without y'all.

To the OGs, the black female officers I have met throughout my journey, especially Teresa, I want to express my gratitude. You may not remember this, but the day you dropped off a printed copy of penal codes with a binder of study material was the day I realized I too, could do this. Your kind gesture did not go unnoticed. I appreciate you! Thank you for being a positive example of a strong, black female officer for me and many others.

Grandma, thank you for being one of my biggest supporters. I love you!

My incredible Godparents (J&J and M&J), who have continuously supported me from day one, thank you. I love you all! To my God Mom (JHE) for taking the time to listen to me share ideas about my book, having faith in my visions, and challenging me to think outside of the box. Thank you!

ECO, thank you for not only encouraging me to share my story but creating a safe space for me to be myself, authentically. For being you, an amazing human being.

BDH, thank you for always rooting for me. For encouraging me to write this book on days I felt like I couldn't and allowing me to run my illustrations by you.

CT, thank you for your honesty, your support, and for encouraging me to be confident in sharing my gift of writing.

To the team at NY Publishers, especially my editing team. Thank you for bringing my first book to life. I truly appreciate you all.

A special thanks to my family, who have kept me lifted up, not only through my journey as a police officer but my journey through life. To my aunts and cousins for constantly checking on me, your "check-in" text messages or calls are always right on time. To my uncles, for your support and constant law enforcement "po-po" jokes, I know I can always count on you guys to make me laugh.

Thank you to those who provided me with the content for this book through experiences, good and bad 😉

To my very powerful circle of strong women, my tribe *(you know who you are)*, I couldn't have done it without you ladies. Thank you for keeping me grounded, always.

Lastly, to all the people who helped bring this book to life in so many other ways, thank you all for being a part of this amazing yet unbelievable journey. Your feedback, big and small, has helped make this book a reality, and for that, I will always be grateful.

I love you!!!